CRACKS IN THE KREMLIN WALL

Also by Edward Crankshaw
RUSSIA AND THE RUSSIANS

CRACKS
in the KREMLIN
WALL

by EDWARD CRANKSHAW

New York, THE VIKING PRESS

1951

PRINTED IN THE UNITED STATES OF AMERICA

BY AMERICAN BOOK–KNICKERBOCKER PRESS, INC., NEW YORK

Contents

v

1. *Communism and Eternal Russia*

1

Who Is the Enemy?

THE FIRST THING to do in any conflict is to define the enemy. Only then can we decide what the conflict is about; and until we know what we are fighting, and why, we shall not get very far. The conflict we are all engaged in now has been in progress for some years. It has passed from what we call the Cold War to military operations in Korea. And even now, at this advanced stage of belligerence, we still have not defined the enemy, which is another way of saying that we still have no clear idea of what we are fighting, and why. This means not only that we are unable to appreciate the strength and weakness of the other side, not only that we do not know who are our allies in the struggle, but also that we cannot fight effectively. To conceal this fantastic state of affairs we make up for lack of definitions by using labels. Sometimes we call the enemy Russia, sometimes Stalinism, more often communism. Most of us use these labels to mean different things.

3

The question of definition may seem academic in the middle of a battle, with people being killed on both sides. But it is precisely in the middle of a battle that one most urgently needs to know enemies from friends. In this particular conflict, as far as military planning is concerned, the main enemy is seen to be Russia: nothing could be simpler. But Russia is also the headquarters of the Cominform, in fact if not in name; therefore the enemy is communism. Many people in Russia, as we shall see, are against communism: therefore, if the enemy is communism, these are our allies. France is our ally; but many Frenchmen are Communists. In this they are our enemies. When we come to the countries of Eastern Europe, to say nothing of Asia, the situation is even more complicated. Tito is a Communist; but he is also our ally against the Cominform. And so on.

Who, then, are our enemies? Who are our friends? Surely it is important to be as clear as we can about these questions? It is important if only to know whom we should hit, and where. It is important also for our own actions to be unequivocal and plain, so that people all over the world can decide for themselves what we stand for, and therefore whose side they are on. It is important, finally, because in answering these questions about others, we shall have to decide what we mean when we speak of "we."

Many people talk today as though Russia and communism were identical; but clearly they are not. Russia is a great power. She has existed a long time and would exist today if there were no such thing as communism. Communism, on the other hand, is a political philosophy, an interpretation of life. A species of socialism based on the dialectical materialism of Marx and Engels would exist today if there were no such place as Russia. We can go further. We can say that even if Marx and Engels had never existed, there would be some sort of revolutionary socialism actively at work in the world today. What has happened, in fact, is that Russia and what we call communism, two facts of life having no intrinsic connection with each other, have become identified with each other, so that to many of us (but not, for example, to Tito) Russia and communism are synonyms. The Moscow government has gone to great lengths to foster this identification.

The reason for this is quite simple. The men who have declared war on our society, the Bolshevik leaders, are the rulers of Russia. Initially, however, they declared war not as the government of a great power, but as the chief exponents of a particular brand of socialism, called bolshevism. If they could identify bolshevism in our eyes with Russia, plainly they would appear to us as being far stronger than their party membership would suggest. But in fact bolshevism has never been the same as Russia, and it is in our own interest to keep them apart in our minds. Indeed, we have to go a step farther: we have to ask whether the men who call themselves Bolsheviks, Stalin and his government, may reasonably be called Communists at all.

This is not word-spinning. It is the most vital question of our time. For reasons which we shall later discuss, the avowed enemies of our society, and the sole avowed enemies apart from certain African and Asiatic nationalist movements, are the government of the Soviet Union, together with what supporters they can muster among the Communist Party of the Soviet Union (with a total membership of six millions) and the devoted affiliates of the Soviet Communist Party in other lands. It is plainly of immense importance to decide whether now, regardless of what may have happened in the past, the Soviet government is fighting us in what it conceives to be the interests of the Soviet Union or in what it conceives to be the interests of revolutionary socialism. This is the sort of question we cannot begin to answer until we have sorted out Russia from communism and communism as it is conceived in the Kremlin from communism as it is conceived in the minds of countless thousands of devoted fighters for the underdog. When we have done this the question will almost certainly answer itself.

Until that question is answered we are liable to go terribly astray. By "we" I do not mean what is all too often known nowadays as Western civilization, which seems to me an unreal concept, or, if real, certainly nothing to be proud of; for the term "Western civilization," if it means anything at all, must include, to come no nearer home, Nazi Germany and Fascist Italy and Falangist Spain. By "we" I mean men and women everywhere, of all parties and all religions, or none, who believe in a liberal and liberalizing tradition, for whatever reasons, and in the need for the rule of law based, as nearly as may be, on certain absolute moral standards, laboriously achieved, and who will resort to force to sustain that rule wherever it may have been achieved, but for no other purpose whatsoever. This seems to me something like the irreducible minimum of what we may be said to stand for; and I do not see how we can stand for less without turning against those things, or for more, except privately as individuals, without demanding forced allegiances in others. To stand for an idea, of course, is not necessarily to live up to it.

It follows from this that we can recognize only one active enemy, and that is the man, or group, or power, which seeks deliberately to overturn by violence or treachery the societies we seek, all too insufficiently, to model on those beliefs. We have to remember that there are different degrees of hostility, and that the difference between some of these degrees is so great as to be a difference in kind. The man who would like to see you dead, but who does nothing active about it, shows a hostility different in kind from that of the man who sets out to kill you. Translate this difference into terms of nations, and we have all the difference between war and peace. The man who would like to kill you but is physically incapable is another sort of enemy, and we usually ignore him. The man who is determined to kill you, but, uncertain of his strength, or fearful of the consequences, is prepared to wait patiently until propitious circumstances arise, is still another sort of enemy. He may die first.

There is only one group of people in the world today which is actively and deliberately, and for whatever reason, committed to the downfall of our society: the group of Russians who form the government of the Soviet Union. This group has allies—allies willing and convinced, forced allies, deluded allies, unconscious allies—in what proportions we do not know. But I think it is fair to say that when we think of the enemy in the great struggle before us we should exclude until the last possible moment all those who are not the convinced and willing allies of the Kremlin. The rest we should seek to detach from the enemy camp by all means in our power, even those who may be fighting us for reasons of their own.

Marshal Tito calls himself a Communist. He dissents from our values as outlined above. If we are to believe him, he would like to see revolution everywhere. But so long as he takes no active steps to forward the cause of revolution by breaking down our existing society he must be free, by our standards, to say what he likes, and in his own country to do what he can. Many decent and honest individuals of all races and creeds call themselves Communists. In so far as they act as conscious agents for Stalin they turn themselves into the active enemies of our society and must be treated as such. In so far as they are consciously upright and unaware of the fact that Stalin is exploiting them for his own purposes they are tiresome nuisances, even dangerous nuisances; but they are no more the active enemies of our society than millions of others whose personal ambitions or ideals make rational government more difficult—perhaps healthily more difficult.

In a word, to confuse the conflict with the Kremlin and a general conflict with what is called communism is to bring us into grave danger. For this confusion is liable to turn our action in what we call the Cold War into a crusade against what we call communism, which all too easily degenerates into a crusade against all those movements, however narrow and misguided, which work in the end for the destruction of the worst abuses of a society by no means perfect. And in so far as this crusade brings us into active conflict with so-called Communists who do not willingly and consciously support the Kremlin's campaign, or who have no intention at all of carrying their own struggle beyond the borders of their own countries, we ourselves are then the aggressors, seeking to impose on other nations our own values, however lofty-seeming, by force of arms. This, I suggest, is the negation of those values.

It seems to me that there is only one way of clarifying this extraordinarily complex subject, and that is by trying to discover what has happened in Russia during the last thirty years and what the Kremlin is aiming at today, and why.

2

The Bolshevik Conspiracy

In IDENTIFYING the Russian Bolsheviks, who are the masters of the Soviet Union, as the enemy, we do no more than take at face value their own declarations. The declared aim of the Bolsheviks is to achieve what they call communism throughout the world by encouraging internal revolutions against established governments, violently conducted. Their authority for this is Karl Marx. The declared policy of the Bolsheviks is to exploit what they call revolutionary situations in other countries and support the insurgents, where it is possible, by Soviet arms or the threat of Soviet arms. Marx said nothing about this, so they have to invoke Lenin for authority here. The declared method whereby the Bolsheviks seek to realize their aim is by undermining the authority and stability of bourgeois governments everywhere and by every conceivable means. Since the government of a sovereign nation is for all international purposes the nation itself, these aims and methods amount to a declaration of

9

war on non-Communist peoples everywhere. The fact that what is commonly known as warlike action may be reserved, or even not contemplated, makes no difference to the principle. War is generally held to be an extension of diplomacy; it is also an extension of Communist strategy, which may or may not be used. Lenin himself made fun of people who try to differentiate between aggressive and defensive war and at the same time said quite unequivocally that world revolution could only ensue after a series of bloody conflicts between nations. Certainly both Lenin and Stalin have also said that there is no reason why the Communist and non-Communist systems should not live peacefully side by side. On the other hand, both have made it clear on many occasions that this "peaceful coexistence" can be no more than temporary; and Stalin has quite recently stated more specifically that even in the Soviet Union the full progress from socialism to communism cannot be completed so long as the "capitalist encirclement" exists. Sooner or later, the final clash must come. As early as 1923, at the Twelfth Party Congress, with Lenin still alive, Stalin produced a handy formula to cover any aggressive war the Soviet Union cared to undertake. As the great champion of national self-determination he was seeking to justify the then recent war against Poland; but his words also set the stage for the North Korean aggression nearly thirty years later:

There are cases when the right of self-determination enters into conflict with another, a higher principle, namely the right of the working class to strengthen its régime once it has achieved power. In such a case—and this must be frankly stated—the right of self-determination cannot and must not serve as a barrier to the realization of the right of the working class to its dictatorship. The first must yield to the second. Such was, for instance, the case in 1920, when we were forced to march on Warsaw in order to defend the power of the working class.

The working class, of course, means the Russian Communist Party.

It may seem odd to call the Bolsheviks the enemy when they are so vociferous in protesting that what they want is peace. We shall examine the contemporary peace movement later under the general head of Soviet propaganda; but for the moment, taking it at its face value, it is worth pointing out its irrelevance. Apologists for the Kremlin invariably assert that all those Soviet actions which we call aggressive are really defensive actions inspired by fear. Up to a point there is some truth in this. But it begs the question.

What sort of peace does the Kremlin want? And why is it afraid? When all is said, the hunted burglar is afraid; but does his fear excuse the further crimes he commits to keep himself at liberty? Even the murderer seeks peace.

The Kremlin is afraid of its own conception of the inevitable clash. This is nothing less than fear of the consequences of its own actions. The Kremlin has taken the offensive against the established systems of the West, and it expects the West to hit back. To reduce the power of the inevitable counteroffensive it increases its onslaught and, in so doing, deepens the risk of military retaliation. This makes the Kremlin still more afraid, and so on to infinity. In a word, the fear of the Soviet government, which is genuine and obsessional, is in part the outcome of what we should call a guilty conscience—except that it runs counter to Bolshevik principles to have a conscience. It is the most difficult sort of fear to dispel, because only the possessor of it knows how deeply justified it is.

The Bolsheviks, of course, with their peculiar conception of history, do not see the picture in this light at all. We, who have an established system to defend, to retain or change in our own good time and manner, can only regard the Bolshevik attack as aggression. But they see in Lenin's revolution and everything that followed the very reverse of aggression: they see it as a counterattack on the entrenched positions of a conquering minority who have had things their own way for too long.

Once the conquering minority and the subject majorities were seen as classes. Now they are seen as nations.

In the days when the Bolsheviks were in exile, or forming an underground resistance to the Tsars, they developed, under Lenin, a code of behaviour. This code was not only the natural expression of a persecuted minority, which takes its weapons where it can find them; it was also the expression of a group of men who called themselves materialists and who subscribed to a materialist conception of history which taught that all values were relative and all morality the protective apparatus of a dominant class in the deadly struggle of conflicting self-interests which was the mainspring of progress. The church, for example, with its moral code, was conjured into being to frighten the poor into proper subservience to the powerful and rich. Religion, seen as the opium of the people, was a spurious comfort for the robbed, who reconciled themselves to their miserable lot with the thought of riches laid up in heaven. Justice was the rich man's citadel. And so on. The fact that religion, church, and justice, together with the whole apparatus of law, order, and morality, have all too frequently been perverted in precisely this way does not make such charges any easier to contradict, especially when they are laid by the kind of fanatic whose idea of logic leads him to believe that because all dogs have tails every animal with a tail must be a dog. Religion, morality, justice, have all been perverted to base ends, sometimes more, sometimes less; therefore they are base. Honesty and truth, so-called moral qualities, have no meaning at all except as aspects of a predatory code designed to keep down the poor. Moral values change to suit the needs of the ruling class of the moment. Thus there are no absolutes in morals. Thus, if it suits the revolutionary to exalt the lie, there can be no question of immorality. And so on.

It did, of course, suit the Bolsheviks, the persecuted minority, to exalt the lie; but because of their conception of morality it was not even incumbent upon them to plead that the means is sanctified by the end—although, so imperfect is the human mind, so human even the man who calls himself a materialist, that many of them did so, quite superfluously. Lenin, however, did not. Never once did he apologize for any of his actions. He was part of a historical drama. The part he played was the part required in the great, amoral, materialist dialectic, and, though forlorn, it had a certain grandeur.

In addition to being a born materialist, Lenin was also a born conspirator. He was also a born Russian. To be a conspiratorial Russian and a natural materialist into the bargain offers unparalleled opportunities for chicanery of every kind. Lenin made the most of them. He would have been a more impressive figure had he been a little less pleased with his own duplicity. The great Bolshevik would be, like the devil or the superman, beyond good and evil and would take no pride in his own deceit, which would be the natural air for him, as for Apollyon. Lenin, for all his gifts, was only a human being, frequently too clever by half, who, intoxicated by his own diabolism, drew attention to it on every possible occasion. Often, indeed, he put himself to great trouble to obtain through deceit what he could quickly have had for the asking.

This, to return, was the atmosphere surrounding the early Bolsheviks, who, naturally, were very much conscious of their own impotence in face of the vast established order of the world, even though they told themselves that the order was doomed. The success of Lenin's revolution was the very last thing they expected; and some of them, indeed, like the Mensheviks, were convinced that Lenin's action was at least a generation too soon. They arrived, that is to say, in the echoing corridors of the Petrine palaces not only with blood on their hands and mud on their boots, but also with fear in their hearts and the mentality of a rather shabby secret society suddenly called upon to govern instead of to plot. For a long time, by sheer force of habit, they went on plotting—against each other, now that they were on top; against rival revolutionary parties; against the bureaucrats on whom they utterly depended. They were saved only by the convergence against them of a powerful force of antirevolutionary Russians, backed and supported by the armies of foreign powers. This force, like the American people today in their opposition to what they call communism, was indiscriminate in its attack. It fought, that is to say, not only the Bolsheviks, who were the only serious menace to decency, but also those millions of common people who, for one reason and another, were against the return of the old régime, thus forcing them into alliance with Lenin, who offered himself as the only leader of value. During this tremendous struggle, the Bolshevik Party found its feet; and when the fighting was over and chaos and famine ruled the stricken land, there

was no one to challenge them at all. They were still conspirators; but now they were conspirators on a wider
front. Their conspiracy was no longer the conspiracy of
a closely articulated party against the established order:
it had become the conspiracy of a group of men against
the people whom they ruled; and, on a different level, the
conspiracy of one government against all other governments. The equipment the Bolsheviks brought to their
conspiracies was the equipment designed to ensure the
survival of a minority party of subversive fanatics and
adventurers, Russians, often Jews, who had plotted fantastically the overthrow of established society in Zurich
and Finsbury Circus, or preached sedition inside the Chinese wall of Tsarist Russia, all the time quarrelling bitterly
among themselves—a party of Russians who had got hold
of a German philosophy of history which provided the
more intelligent of them with an intellectual armoury and
the less intelligent with an excuse to conduct themselves
like pedantic thugs and call the result historical necessity.

It was in this atmosphere that the tactics and strategy
of bolshevism were developed (and nothing is more important than to keep the tactics and strategy, on the one
hand, and the ultimate aims, on the other, apart in one's
mind). The Bolsheviks have always thought of themselves
as a minority party in bitter struggle for their existence
and hated, for good reason, by the rest of the world. The
senior members of the government of the U.S.S.R. cannot
escape from this conception, even today, although they
have long since grown away from their early principles.
Whether the new men, who have been brought up to
positions of power inside a strong Russia, are frightened
to the same extent remains to be seen; but it is fair to say
that the whole outlook of the party as such, in Russia as
elsewhere, is conditioned by the fact that it brings to the

technique of government the lamentable tricks of the underdog. Most of its members, at the beginning, did not believe in their power. Some, like Kamenev and Zinoviev, thought they should wait for a further instalment of the Marxist cycle to unfold before they tried to seize it. Others, like Lenin, regarded the October Revolution as a rehearsal, a symbolic act on the lines of the Paris Commune, doomed in advance, but a necessary step in the Bolshevik progress. When the power which, in Lenin's phrase, they picked up from the street after the failure of Kerensky's government, remained with them, it seems temporarily to have misted over their appreciation of the world situation. Lenin, for example, thinking for once in terms of pure Marxism, never expected intervention by the Western powers. When these did intervene, instead of seeing their action as the muddled, convulsive effort of a hardly pressed alliance to prevent a bunch of ragamuffins from concluding on the part of Russia a separate peace with Germany, Lenin at once knew what it was all about. This was an imperial war. Russia was the weakest link in the imperial chain, and the efforts of the Allies to repair it were all part of the Marxist dialectic, as already amended by Lenin. Henceforth the capitalist powers could be relied upon to attack Bolshevik Russia by every conceivable means and on every possible occasion.

The general proposition of the proletarian revolution is based in the Marxist dialectic. In a purely material universe, the unique driving-force is self-interest. The strong, who succeed in acquiring in one way and another more of their fair share of this world's goods, band themselves together to protect their acquisitions and so become a ruling class which sets the pattern of the whole society. All the institutions of a given society, from its church to its law, are devised more or less consciously to protect and strengthen the ruling class and exploit the oppressed classes. But nothing stands still. Everything carries within it the seeds of its own decay. The more perfectly organized the system the more marked the internal balances and tensions. Sooner or later acute contradictions and pressures are felt and the existing system collapses beneath the impact of the very forces it has called into being to assist its own development. Thus, for example, the aristocratic feudal society gave way to its antithesis, the mercantile bourgeois society, which was to develop capitalism. And thus the bourgeois capitalist society must give way to its own antithesis, a society ruled by the oppressed labourers and artisans. This interplay of opposites is seen by the Marxist as an iron law of history. The proletarian society, however, is to be the final phase, the ultimate synthesis, because at last the great masses, as opposed to sectional interests, will have taken over mass control: there will then be no more classes, and therefore no more conflicts of self-interest.

Put like that, it does not sound very good. But we have to remember that Marx was writing at a moment in history when, because of the industrial revolution, the capitalists, the factory owners, were able to exploit the workers to a degree unprecedented since the days of slavery. The gulf between the conquering minority and the subservient majority had been rapidly growing; there was a revolutionary ferment in the air; and Marx saw no reason why the process should be arrested or diverted until it had ended in a smash.

He was wrong. First, for example, he failed to see that, as Professor Carr has put it, the capitalist system had created an immense network of vested interests in its own stability, the small men, who preferred to take their chance of bettering themselves inside the existing system rather than throw the system down and start again. Secondly, he failed to see that there could be no final synthesis, since, even if the proletarian revolution should take place as predicted, humanity would still be divided into the strong and the weak, who would once more range themselves into the exploiters and the exploited, as has happened in Russia since 1917. The fact remains that, his revolutionary theory apart, Marx's thinking has deeply affected the best political and economic thinking of our time; and, paradoxically, it would have affected it a very great deal more had not a group of Russians concentrated on his revolutionary theory and deluded themselves that they had succeeded in turning it into practice.

When Lenin arrived on the scene it was obvious to any-one with a spark of common sense that the Marxist theory of revolution had gone wrong. Lenin himself saw that something had to be done about it, and his own outstanding contribution to Marxist thought, which Stalin has inherited, was the particular proposition which laid down the way in which the proletarian revolution would be achieved.

Marx had believed that sooner or later the proletarian revolution would sweep the world. But he also believed that each country would have to produce its own revolution, which, though accelerated by the international solidarity of the working class, could only occur at a particular point in its development and in its own way. It could never happen until a given country had been through the stage of capitalist development. The Russian Social Democrats in exile, both Bolsheviks and Mensheviks, by and large believed this: it meant in their eyes that Russia must have a bourgeois revolution before they could even begin to contemplate the proletarian revolution. This was not good enough for Lenin. Russia was admittedly at the very bottom of the list of countries ripe for proletarian revolution because she was a backward country with little capitalism, an insignificant proletariat, and a horde of illiterate peasants barely emerged from the feudal stage. Lenin had to justify within the Marxist canon the promotion of Russia to be first on the list, and so he had to extend the Marxist canon. He did this by discovering that times had changed since Marx's day. Then the unit of capitalist society had been the self-contained bourgeois state, like Britain or Germany. Now, owing to the development of imperialism, which involved the exploitation of whole peoples by whole peoples (instead of, as hitherto, classes by classes within nations), the whole situation had altered: a capitalist state could postpone revolution at home by raising the standard of living of the masses with the fruits of colonial oppression. Lenin thus arrived at the following inspired conclusion of *post hoc* argument:

> The West European capitalist countries are consummating their development towards socialism not . . . by the gradual "maturing" of socialism, but by the exploitation of some countries by others, by the exploitation of the first of the countries to be vanquished in the imperialist war (i.e., Russia) combined with the exploitation of the whole of the East. On the other hand, precisely as a result of the first imperialist war, the East has been definitely drawn into the general maelstrom of the world revolutionary movement.

In a word, Lenin had transferred Marx's teaching on the class struggle, a teaching which was visibly breaking down, from the domestic to the international arena. The exploiters and exploited ceased to be classes and became nations. In so doing, he not only explained the Russian Revolution ("the snapping of the weakest link in the imperialist chain") in quasi-Marxist terms, but he also gave the Soviet Union, *as a power,* as the first base of the world revolution, a pretext for intervening in the internal affairs of other powers and indulging in what Mr. Bevin has stigmatized as the most abominable international crime: the fomenting of civil wars as an instrument of policy. He not only brought communism into Russia. Far more importantly, he brought Russia into communism.

3

Marx in Russian Dress

I T WAS LENIN'S NEW DOCTRINE, the imperialist thesis, which turned the Russian Bolsheviks, a seedy lot, into the declared enemies of established society everywhere and at all times. It was the success of Lenin's revolution, much to his own surprise, and the consequent subjugation of all Russia by the Bolsheviks which put the weapon into their hands and made them formidable. Without Russia, that is to say, their hostility would be unavailing; without the imperialist thesis, which was not a part of Marxism, it would have been diffuse and often passive. It was Lenin, and nobody else but Lenin, who gave the Bolsheviks their policy and their teeth; and it is important to remember this, for an understanding of what has happened since, at a time when Lenin has been sentimentalized out of all recognition and all the evils in the world laid directly at Stalin's door. Stalin has produced his own evils, which we shall consider in due course; but these grew naturally, and perhaps inevitably, from Leninism.

Marx in his own way was unscrupulous. He delighted in wars because he thought they would bring his revolution closer. He prayed for the rise of capitalism in backward areas, regardless of the misery he believed it would cause, so that his monstrous dialectic might lurch ponderously into its final lap and bring with it the proletarian revolution to sweep capitalism away. He was Machiavellian in his tactics and spiteful in his temper. But compared with Lenin he was as innocent as the day. His idea of a war, for example, was a fight for markets between Germany and England; and the historical purpose of such a war was to weaken the capitalist structure and augment the discontent of the workers. What he certainly never in his most malevolent dreams envisaged was the spectacle of a socialist state making war on a capitalist state in order to spread, with the weapons of imperialism, the blessings of communism. Still less did he foresee the deliberate exploitation of the nationalist aspirations of the backward races to embarrass the capitalist system. It took Lenin to think up that sort of thing. It took, that is to say, the impact of a Russian statesman on the ideas of a German professor. The Russianness of Lenin has never, I think, been properly appreciated, and least of all by Lenin himself. But it is the most important thing in the world to appreciate it, because, had Lenin not been a Russian of the Russians, communism as we think of it today, the mortal enemy, simply would not exist.

When the Bolsheviks seized power, almost without bloodshed (that came afterwards), in October 1917, they found themselves translated from professional revolutionaries living underground or in exile into the rulers of a great land. At first they were uncertain rulers, and the land was in chaos. But from the beginning they had to adapt their Marxism to situations which Marx had not foreseen.

The Second International had collapsed under the stress of patriotic emotions everywhere in 1914. The Third was created to carry on its purest traditions. It was created by the Bolsheviks and, with its headquarters in Russia, it was a Bolshevik monopoly. It was known as the Communist International, or Comintern. Its first head was Zinoviev. And it is a measure of the confusion of ideas obtaining among the Bolsheviks at that time that the Comintern was soon at loggerheads with the new Soviet foreign office, or People's Commissariat for Foreign Affairs. In other words, the interests of the Soviet Union as a power very soon came into conflict with the interests of world revolution.

Theoretically, the Communist International should have been a supranational government, a sort of world government of Communists everywhere, with "Workers of the World, Unite!" as its slogan. It should have transcended the domestic government of the Soviet Union and given orders to the Communist Party of the U.S.S.R. no less overriding than its orders to the Communist Parties of France or Ecuador. In fact, it rapidly became an instrument of Soviet foreign policy, of the Soviet foreign office. The conflict between national interests and world revolutionary interests had to be resolved. The resolution, which took some years, naturally and inevitably ended with the subordination of world revolution strategy to Soviet security, with the gloss that the U.S.S.R. was the base and citadel of revolution everywhere.

Theoretically the Russian Bolsheviks were stateless, and Petrograd, and then Moscow, were no more than provisional headquarters of a world-wide movement. Theoretically the various national delegates to the Comintern were equal, which meant that, for example, the voices of the leading German Communists should have carried as much weight in the councils of the Russian Communist

Party as the voices of the Russians in the councils of the German Communist Party. In fact, they did not. The Russian Bolsheviks, who had carried out a successful revolution and possessed themselves of a territorial base, ran the whole show. The predominance of the Russians was to some extent disguised by the fact that Russia had technically ceased to exist. What took its place was the Union of Soviet Socialist Republics, which coincided with much of the territory of the former Russian Empire, but which was seen only as the nucleus of a world-embracing union.

Meanwhile the Soviet Union, which happened to be Russia, had to survive as the base of world proletarian revolution. And soon, after a number of lighthearted excursions, by far the greater part of the energies of the Bolsheviks was devoted to ensuring that survival—the survival, that is to say, of the Soviet Union as a power among other powers. In spite of the pressures of the intervention, this did not happen at once. The Bolsheviks hoped great things of Germany and tried also to carry their system to Poland and Finland by war and to China by civil war. But gradually they went over to the defensive. In 1921, under Lenin, they went over to the defensive in face of the Russian people, making far-reaching concessions to anti-Communist feeling under the New Economic Policy, which permitted private trading. In 1938, under Stalin, they went over to the defensive in face of the outer world, abandoning for the time being all ideas of revolutionary advance. Under the slogan "Socialism in One Country" they sacrificed the immediate prospects of world revolution to the security of the Soviet Union as a power. At the same time, by going over to the defensive in the international sphere, they were able to concentrate their forces for a renewed and final onslaught on the Russian people, who were by no means yet subdued.

By the time the Russian people had been dealt with and the country put through a dizzy industrial revolution— by the end, that is to say, of the second Five-Year Plan in 1938, the base had been consolidated and fortified and the Bolsheviks could once more take an active interest in the larger world, a world at that time shivering in the shadow of the Nazi menace. The process was completed whereby a group of revolutionaries starting as enemies of a social system, the capitalist system wherever it was found, had been transformed into a powerful enemy of whole nations. This development, as we have said, was not foreseen by Marx, who, in any case, never offered a blueprint for a Socialist state, but only for the preliminary revolution. It was not even foreseen by Lenin, who was unable to visualize the establishment and sustenance of a Socialist Russia unless some of her important neighbours could also carry out successful revolutions. But, although Lenin did not foresee, during the chaos of the early years he was adapting himself to unexpected situations with energy and skill, and even while uttering warnings about the dangers of renewed Great Russian chauvinism (warnings, incidentally, directed specifically at Stalin), he himself was making it inevitable. In a sense he was correct in his assumption that the revolution could not succeed in Russia unless there were neighbouring revolutions to keep it company. For the Russian Revolution, as envisaged by Lenin, did not in fact succeed and will never succeed; it has changed into something quite different. But the change was already in full swing while Lenin was still in charge. It had ceased to be the Marxist proletarian revolution and had become the Russian industrial revolution, which had nothing in common with the projected revolutions of the capitalist West beyond the Marxist jargon. In a certain sense, indeed, Lenin's revolution has turned out to be much closer to the earlier bourgeois revolutions of the West, translated into terms of Russia, than to the proletarian revolutions predicated by Marx, none of which, it is worth remarking, has yet taken place anywhere in the world.

The confusion is caused by the fact that this revolution was carried out by people who thought they were making a Marxist revolution. There is no reason at all why Russia should not have carried out some sort of revolution without involving herself in uncompromising enmity with the outside world. Later on, we shall have to ask why Lenin, the leader of a fraction of a minority revolutionary party, succeeded where others failed. For the moment, it is enough to say that he did succeed and that implicit in his imperialist thesis, whereby, as we have seen, he transferred the class struggle from a domestic to an international arena, was the situation whereby Communist powers would find themselves ranged in deadly and belligerent opposition to anti-Communist powers, so that world revolution could only be achieved through a series of bloody conflicts between nations.

It is important to remember that no other Left-wing group, or party, has ever thought in these terms. It is a line of thought peculiar to the Russian Social Democrats alone. Even the Menshevik wing of the Russian Social Democrats did not think in those terms. This means that the Russian Bolshevik Party, later misleadingly called Communist, is the only revolutionary party ever to have declared war on nations, as distinct from classes. And the purpose in emphasizing this point is that, as far as declarations go, the enemy is not socialism, as such, which may sometimes (as in Yugoslavia) be called communism, but bolshevism, or Moscow communism alone, together with what forces it may be able to argue, persuade, dupe, or conscript into its own camp. Thus, in assessing the strength of the enemy,

we have to ask to what extent the Kremlin leaders dispose
of convinced support in whatever they may do among the
Russian people, among the peoples of Russia's satellites,
among the Communist Parties and fellow travellers elsewhere, among the backward peoples with nationalist
aspirations in Asia, Africa, and South America. We also
have to ask to what extent the Kremlin leaders still believe
in Leninism.

4

The Hands of Esau

THE FIRST STEP towards a just appreciation of the enemy's strength is to sort out, as best we may, Russianism from what we call communism. When they seized power the Bolsheviks ceased to be persecuted revolutionaries in themselves. They were the rulers of Russia and, because of them, Russia became a persecuted country. This naturally confirmed the Bolsheviks in their conspiratorial ways, above all as expressed in the Comintern. Simultaneously, reacclimatization to the atmosphere of Russia brought out the Russian in them. So that today we are faced no longer with a hostile group of Bolsheviks who happened to be Russians, but by a hostile group of Russians who happen to be Bolsheviks and who have more or less refashioned the government of a great power in their own image.

Nowadays it is generally accepted that in many ways the Stalin régime has become heavily coloured by traditional Russianism. During the war, particularly, it was commonly believed that the old traditions had quite swallowed up the Marxist ideology, a belief that has now been largely abandoned. In fact, we were nearer the truth than we now realize. Certainly the Russianism of the Kremlin is something quite other, and far deeper, than a preoccupation with military insignia, archbishops, and tsarist saints and heroes—all these being the obvious stock in trade of any Russian government trying to get on the right side of the people during a major national crisis. The Russianism of the Kremlin is older than Stalin's régime. I have already suggested that it was imported by Lenin himself; and the extent to which the revolutionary socialism was in fact Russianized by Lenin was so great that it forms an excellent way into our subject.

The popular conception of Lenin, which was shared by Lenin himself, is that he was the supreme type of international revolutionary. The popular conception of Stalin is that he is the great betrayer of Lenin's particular kind of Marxism, called bolshevism. In fact, all that Stalin has done, as I shall try to show, is to carry Leninism to its logical conclusion. And this logical conclusion is farther away from Marxism than most people are ready to believe. It could, indeed, be best described as anti-Marxism. This, I believe, is not a betrayal of Lenin; it is, rather, an exposure of Lenin, who should, I think, be seen as a Russian first and a Marxist afterwards.

At the moment all the evils in Russia are attributed to Stalin always, and sometimes to Lenin as a Bolshevik (according to the political beliefs of the critic), but never to Lenin as a Russian. The propaganda for this view is powerful, and it speaks with many voices. It is put out by Russians who disapprove of both Lenin and Stalin, like Kerensky; by Russian and foreign Communists who disapprove of Stalin, like Trotsky and Tito; by foreigners who approve of the Russian people but cannot stomach their government; and by lapsed Communists, Russians like Kravchenko and foreigners like Koestler and Burnham. All these voices, together with those of practically all White Russian exiles, have one thing in common: good personal reasons for proving that the evils which now afflict Russia and the world are Stalin's evils (and sometimes Lenin's too) and never Russian evils.

Certainly Stalin has done many things which Lenin did not do, many other things which Lenin would not have done had he lived. But it is of the very first importance in any assessment of the conflict in which we are now caught up to realize that the critical part of what Stalin has done was inherent in Lenin's ideas and practices, and that these ideas and practices were as much a product of Russia as they were of Marx and Engels. Lenin would have been cleverer than Stalin and, within limits, more flexible. He might, therefore, have avoided some of the mistakes which Stalin made and had to pay for with untold vicarious suffering. But sooner or later, had he lived, Lenin would have been forced along Stalin's way—or to resignation or suicide.

Certainly, also, Lenin was able to impose upon the long-suffering people of Russia a form of central tyranny by a minority which the majority deeply resented. But it is one of the purposes of this book to show that, given the abdication of the tsar and the March Revolution (neither of which owed anything to Lenin), an absolute dictatorship of some kind was inevitable. The March Revolution was not carried out by Lenin, who was then in Switzerland, or by his party, which was then impotent: it was carried out by the Russian people, manipulated by commercial interests soon swept away by the flood they let loose, who then, in the classical Russian manner, did not know what to do.

But this time the Russian people had gone a long step further than in their previous convulsive revolts against oppression: they had got rid of the central autocracy, which created an intolerable vacuum. This vacuum had to be filled, and Lenin filled it.

If this is true, as I think we shall find it to be, it follows that the Bolshevik régime is a natural product of Russia—though by no means the only possible product. This is a statement which anti-Soviet Russians object to very strongly. When we come to look at the Soviet system in detail it will be easy to appreciate their feelings. But even the established fact that many millions of Russians detest their régime is irrelevant. Hitler was a natural product of Germany, yet many Germans loathed him. The Whitehall bureaucracy, as perfected by the Labour government, is a natural product of England; yet a great many of us detest it and sincerely believe that it is strangling England. To cry out against the consequences of our own actions does not absolve us of all responsibility for them.

We shall have more to say later on about the Russian character. It is brought in here only to support the suggestion that the present régime in Russia has an organic connection with the Russian people, no matter how bitterly they may groan beneath it. The Soviet régime is a Russian response to a Russian situation. The acceptance of a detested régime by the people is a Russian response to a Russian situation: governments in Russia are made to be detested. Obviously this simple generalization does not in the least imply that the Soviet régime is the only possible response; nor does it apply to every individual. Far from it. But it does apply to the masses of Russians, who really are masses (Lenin was right about that). And should these words come into the hands of any Russian, outraged by the suggestion that the Soviet labour laws or the prison camps

of Mr. Beria owe their existence not only to an unscrupulous dictatorship but also to the nature of the most spontaneous, genial, and feckless people in the world, then he
is invited to consider the following two questions: Can he
honestly imagine the Russian peasant responding to anything at all but loving-kindness or naked force? And has
any government in history anywhere been able to operate
through loving-kindness?

If it is possible to see in the Soviet régime a reflection,
no matter how distorted and foreshortened, of the Russian
people, what is far clearer and less equivocal is the influence of the traditional Russian governing technique on
Lenin's thought and action.

Russia as a world power has worried us for over two
centuries, for one century acutely. She would be worrying
us very much today, communism or no communism—an
immense and unfathomable power following an almost
sleepwalking habit of expansion along the line of least resistance, and propelled by a chaos of motives ranging from
a pathological obsession with security to a sombre arrogance, expressing itself in a profound but ill-defined conviction that it is the Russian mission to save the world
from itself. The obsession with security manifests itself
particularly in a horror of anything like a power vacuum.
Today, when the power vacuum is the most conspicuous
feature on the map of the world, Russia, in any shape or
form, would be making hay. But we could cope with that
in terms of simple power politics. Communism, on the
other hand, or some sort of revolutionary socialism, going
hand in hand with revolutionary nationalism, would also
be very much a feature of our age, Russia or no Russia, a
worrying feature. It did not, for example, require Moscow
to set the Far East on fire.

Or, conversely, a reactionary tsarist Russia would still

know how to profit by the nationalist unrest in the Far East and turn it to her own ends. In fact, she did this fairly successfully in the days before the revolution.

What makes the situation so formidable is precisely the combination of a natural revolutionary movement all over the world and an expansive power which, by identifying itself with this movement, is able to profit by it, and, in varying degrees, to guide it and control it. An expansive power, moreover, in the hands of men who believe that sooner or later their system must conquer the world or be conquered.

On the other hand, although it is the combination of Russia, bolshevism, and the revolutionary spirit all over the world which gives us our too frequent sense of hopelessness, there is another side to the picture. If, as I believe, Leninism is largely a particular perversion of Russianism, it can only mean that it is affected by all the essentially Russian characteristics, including the Russian's attitude towards war and foreign policy; and the Russian national character thus assumes very great importance in modifying Bolshevik logic. Similarly, the strength of the Soviet régime, such as it is, is dependent on the fact that Stalinism has an organic connection with the Russian people. There is certainly no such connection between Stalinism and the East European satellite people, or China, to say nothing of the non-Russian peoples of the U.S.S.R. Finally, the very ease with which the Kremlin has made its postwar advances may tend to its undoing. For Russia is still the country which, given half a chance, bites off more than it can chew; and the Soviet régime, as we have suggested, is still essentially a Russian régime, of the kind which is tolerable to Russians but, as far as can be seen, to no other people on earth.

But we are getting on to dangerous ground. That is to

say, we approach the fringe of what has come to be known
as wishful thinking; and since it is likely to happen again
(since the main purpose of this book is to suggest that the
enemy, while far from having feet of clay, is not so formidable as he looks, seen looming through the mists of
half the world), perhaps a digression is in order.

If in the course of the present conflict we go to our
downfall, this will be due very largely to fear of two
catchwords. The first is "wishful thinking"; the second
"appeasement." This fear is paralysing our minds. We are
so afraid of wishful thinking that many of us have stopped
thinking altogether, in case we think a wishful thought.
We are so afraid of appeasement that many of us have
quite forgotten that agreement is the whole basis of society, and that agreement may include any kind of coming together, whether permanent or provisional, whether
based on conviction or on opportunism (we cannot dictate
other people's motives), whether in all sincerity or with
hindthought. . . . And to those who say that, for example,
Russia does not want a lasting agreement, that she com-
promises only to leap further next time, that any agreement she makes is no more than a tactical manœuvre, the
answer is, surely, So what? It is quite possible for the
Kremlin to decide that its ultimate preposterous ideal can
best be attained by a *détente,* by the cultivation of peace
and goodwill for a period of years. What is, then, the
reality? The substance of peace or the shadow of ultimate
conflict?

As for wishful thinking—this is rapidly coming to include all thinking towards the attainment of a desired
end: purposeful thinking, that is to say. In the context of
our present conflict, if Russia is strong and united, as is
commonly believed; if her hold on the satellites is as absolute as is commonly believed; if she will be able to domi-

nate the Asiatic, African, and South American revolutionary movements, as is commonly believed; and if she is
really intent on achieving physical world domination
within a measurable time, as is commonly believed—then
there is no hope for us short of a total war. Certainly in
such a situation there is no place for thought, but only for
a blind, convulsive effort. Perhaps that is what we should
be doing. Perhaps we should be dropping atom bombs on
the cities of Russia on one of these fine nights to make a
bonfire which will allay our fears of the dark—until the
fire burns down and the darkness returns. That is a point
of view, but not, I think, a very good point of view. In
which case the only other way is to assess the danger and,
by trying to make some sort of appreciation of the enemy
strength and weakness, as well as his real intentions, clear
the way for a practical plan of campaign. It is useless to
make an appreciation of the strength while leaving the
weakness out of account; but that is what our fear of
wishful thinking is perpetually making us do. Just as our
fear of appeasement is leading us to rule out all attempts
at diplomacy, all efforts at negotiation in detail, in case
we should lose on the deal. Men of business, one understands, are out to get the best of each bargain. To this end
they negotiate, knowing perfectly well that each would
happily bankrupt the other if he had half a chance. But
present-day statesmen, who are supposed to breathe a
purer air, have reached the point when any concession is
regarded as the deadly sin.

To return. What Lenin, who thought he was as international as a *wagon-lit,* imported into Marxism was, precisely, Russianism. He was a Russian of the central plain,
and he thought like one. Perhaps the thing that strikes
the Western liberal most about communism (and it is on
this rock that most Western Communists have broken) is

its shattering and soul-destroying cynicism, and particularly the way in which, time without end, it shows that
it is never content until it has corrupted its own agents
into mindless functionaries. This is sometimes taken as
certain proof that the rulers of Russia believe in nothing
at all and are interested only in keeping power—in a word,
that they are unprincipled gangsters. How easy, as already
observed, it would be if they were! Gangsters are vulnerable in many ways. But they are more than that. The tsars,
and many of their most gifted advisers, behaved towards
their agents precisely in the way in which the Politburo
behaves towards its own. But the tsars were not autocratic
gangsters concerned only with their own personal gain.
They believed with passion in the greatness and glory of
Russia and, against all the evidence, in her destiny as the
saviour of the world. They were prepared to take risks in
the service of this belief, and this made them difficult to
handle. And yet they never for one moment saw that their
extraordinary incapacity to trust their subordinates and
subjects until they had been corrupted into submission
was precisely what lay behind Russia's backwardness and
her failure to live up to their dreams. The Russian has
always preferred the venal servant to the upstanding servant. The extraordinary fascination of the Canadian Blue
Book about the Ottawa spy investigation lies in the spectacle of the Soviet officials, on orders from Moscow, deliberately corrupting loyal and idealistic fellow travellers.
It was not enough for a Moscow agent to have Miss X.
handing him Canadian government secrets because of a
convinced belief in the righteousness of the Soviet cause.
A young woman with a convinced belief in anything is
dangerous. She may change her belief. The only prudent
thing to do, even if it means breaking her heart, even if it
means reducing her efficiency, is to trap her into accepting

the train fare from Ottawa to Montreal and get a signed receipt for the money received. And then you have got her forever. And so this was done. And so the agents of the tsars did in their day. The atmosphere of the Canadian Blue Book, of Igor Gouzenko's tale of his escape from the Soviet Legation and the subsequent sacking of his rooms by the N.K.V.D., of Mrs. Kasenkina's account of what happened to her after her first escape from the Soviet Consulate in New York—is the atmosphere of nineteenth-century Russia, changed only by the technical apparatus of the twentieth century and the added intensity of the new ideology. The crushingly cynical passages in Conrad's *Secret Agent* and *Under Western Eyes* are being repeated day after day, as we live, in all the capitals of the world and in every village of the Soviet Union and its satellites. Councillor Mikulin confronting the student Razumov with his bleak, unanswerable "Where to?" when the poor wretch announces his departure; the abominable Mr. Vladimir with his mixture of total clumsiness and total ruthlessness, instructing Mr. Verloc in the elements of imbecile destructiveness—these are the characters of every day wherever communism reaches. It is not communism. It is Russia. Or, rather, official Russia. Just as the tsars tried to kill the spirit of self-respect, upon which the realm depended, so the Soviet government is deliberately killing the spirit of communism, because it is afraid of the spirit of communism, as all Russian governments have been afraid of every vital spirit, everywhere.

We saw it happen in Russia. More recently we have seen it happening in Eastern Europe. Moscow did not, for example, try to win over the Czechs to communism by appealing to their finer feelings: it won them over by appealing to their basest feelings—once it had them in its grip. Moscow does not want an army of militant Communist idealists. Militant idealists are dangerous. So Moscow uses these to do its initial work for it, to close the net —and then denounces them as American agents and kills them.

It was Lenin who injected this spirit into Marxism, not Stalin. Just as it was Lenin who evolved the imperialist thesis, which has turned communism into one of the nastiest games in the history of the world. This elaboration of Marx, or deviation from Marx, already outlined, is a key to the whole of Soviet behaviour. It also reflects an essentially Russian angle on the world situation. It invites the use of essentially Russian tactics, which thus become Communist tactics.

Nothing could be more beneficial to those who think that the Communist technique of infiltration and corruption is something new than to take a short course in Russian history. To be up to date, the triangular relationship between Russia, China, and Japan between 1850 and 1914 would do excellently for a start.

For example, in 1912, when Germany was trying to persuade Russia to cooperate in strengthening China against Japan, China then visibly disintegrating, the Russian foreign minister, Sazonov, could reply:

> Germany is interested in China's buying power and she fears China's disintegration. . . . Russia, on the contrary, as a nation bordering on China, and a long unfortified frontier, cannot wish for a strengthening of her neighbour; she could therefore quietly witness the downfall of modern China.

Thus, too, Soviet Russia—until the time came to strengthen Communist China as an ally against America.

Again, Krupensky, one of those energetic and intriguing Russian envoys who could be relied upon to work for the glory of Imperial Russia with all the assiduity of a Communist envoy working for the glory of Stalin, reported back on the situation produced by the idea of an international loan to put China on her feet:

> We must see to it that China remains in her present state of helplessness as long as possible. Either the loan must not materialize at all, or else it must be tied up with foreign control and supervision in such a way that it will arouse the indignation of the people. The acceptance of such conditions by a central government will lead to disorders in the provinces and perhaps even to an uprising in the south of China.

So Mr. Molotov must have spoken to his colleagues in the Kremlin about the threat of the Marshall Plan to stabilize Western Europe. . . .

Again, when in 1911 the whole of Russian policy in China was jeopardized by the institution of the consortium of the powers, another device to bolster up China, Russia decided to enter the consortium for the sole purpose of opposing from within any action opposed to her own interests and, if need be, to paralyse it completely. This procedure, too, has a familiar ring. . . .

Again, when China allowed Russia to put an armed guard on the Chinese Eastern Railway and first leased her a belt of land along the railway, then permitted her to station guards along its length, the next thing that happened was that in the Russian enclave the city of Harbin was built, and from it Russian officials, disguised as railway functionaries, were soon effectively governing Manchuria, backed by a force of thirty thousand railway police.

These instances could be multiplied. Nor is the similarity between Lenin and Stalin, on the one hand, and the tsars, on the other, confined to method. The motives,

too, are not unlike. Imperial Russia, that is to say, did not
drive into the Far East for economic motives. She despised the preoccupation of what she called the trading
nations with markets and commercial prosperity. Just as
in the sixteenth century Ivan the Terrible had bitterly re-
proached Elizabeth of England, with whom he sought an
alliance, for thinking of nothing but her merchants and
thus showing herself unfit to be a queen, so the later tsars
rejected with sombre loathing the commercial aspirations
of the West and exalted the chaos of dynamic impulses
already mentioned into a mystique of pure glory.

Later on we shall have to consider in detail this extremely important aspect of the Russian approach to imperialism. Meanwhile it is perhaps not extravagant to
suggest that the fervour with which the Russian Bolsheviks
have adopted the Marxist conception of the innate doom
of a society built upon unrestricted trade rather more
than echoes the high and mighty contempt of Ivan and
Boris and Feodor for the driving force which carried
Tudor seamen to find the Northwest Passage and Cathay.

Finally, the theoretical writing of Lenin and the whole
tactic and strategy of bolshevism are deeply coloured by
Russian habits of mind; and the all-or-nothing absolutism,
which Marx so much despised in the tsarist statesmen (as
well as in the obscure "Russian comrades" of his heyday)
lay behind the cynicism of Lenin's party line. The technique of Stalin's policy is implicit in the following words
of Lenin, which might themselves, with changed references, have been the words of any tsarist foreign minister
of the nineteenth century:

It is possible to conquer a powerful enemy only by
exerting the most intense effort, by taking thorough,
attentive, meticulous and skilful advantage of each and

every split among the bourgeois of the various countries, and by taking advantage of every opportunity, even the most trivial, to gain a mass ally, though this ally may be temporary and unstable, vacillating, conditional, and unreliable.

The whole of Stalin's infiltration technique is beautifully reflected in the following instructions issued by Trotsky, under Lenin, to a Communist agitation group dispatched to the Ukraine to combat the separatist influence of the Hetman Petloura during the Ukrainian struggle for independence, which, for a time, succeeded in the early days of the revolution. They are also in the spirit of the tsarist penetration of Mongolia and Manchuria:

The arguments we discuss here in Russia with perfect frankness can only be whispered in the Ukraine. . . . It will therefore be your duty to observe the following precepts:

1. Do not force communism upon the Ukrainian peasants until our power is stabilized in the Ukraine.

2. Set about the cautious introduction of communism on the old estates in the guise of cooperative associations.

3. Do your best to make people believe that Russia is not really Communist at all.

4. To take the wind out of Petloura's sails, insist that Russia is all for the independence of the Ukraine, provided she agrees to set up a Soviet government.

5. Only a fool would go about shouting from the housetops that the Soviet government is fighting Petloura. Sometimes it will be advisable even to set the rumour going that in fact we are in alliance with

Petloura, at any rate until Denikin is finally liquidated.

And so on. Only a few words here and there would have
to be changed to turn these words of Lenin's chief assist-
ant into a replica of the directives which must have been
issued by Georgi Malenkov to the prospective heads of
the East European puppet governments waiting in Moscow, in 1945, for the order to go over the top. In this way,
too, Outer Mongolia was detached from China by the
tsarist envoys in 1912.

"I am aware," wrote the assiduous Krupensky from
Pekin in 1912, "that we cannot openly act against the
wishes of a friendly France and England. . . . Thus I never
speak out frankly to my colleagues . . . in order not to
divulge the task that I have set myself, which is to hinder
the creation of a China organized on European or Japanese models."

5

Despotism and the Russian People

IT MAY BE ARGUED that this sort of crude Machiavellism
which distinguished the policies both of the tsars and of
Lenin is not peculiar to Russia. Candour is not a feature
of diplomacy anywhere in the world, and although the
tsarist foreign office showed the way to Lenin and Stalin
in making a virtue of falsity, this, it could be said, was
only carrying to the logical conclusion a universal diplomatic practice. If that is conceded, more than half the case
for the continuity of tsarist and Soviet practice falls to
the ground. We shall have to agree either that there is
nothing in common between the deceptions of Molotov
and the deceptions of Gorchakov, or else that these deceptions do not differ in kind from the deceptions of all foreign ministers everywhere.

But it cannot be conceded. There is a difference in kind
between the Russo-Soviet ideal of duplicity *à l'outrance*
and the highly variable *ad hoc* duplicity of the West, a
difference which reflects a basic difference of attitude—the

43

attitude not only of statesmen but also of the peoples. And here, in order to get into perspective the actions of Russian statesmen, who do not function in a vacuum, we must begin to take into consideration the people from whom they spring.

I have already suggested the existence of a profound organic connection between the Soviet régime and the people of Russia (we are speaking of Great Russia here, the real master of all the republics of the Soviet Union); and it is time to elaborate a little. First, however, let it be said again that in stressing the Russian characteristics of bolshevism, in suggesting tsarist precedents for practices which we have come to regard as quintessentially Communist practices, nothing is further from my mind than any desire to suggest that the Soviet régime is the inevitable expression of the Russian people or that the people as a whole are ardent supporters of the Soviet régime. Later on in this book I shall be suggesting just the opposite. Further, the Russian flavour of the Soviet régime is a weakness in perhaps more ways than it is a source of strength.

There is, nevertheless, a profound opposition between the natural Russian way of life and the natural Anglo-Saxon way of life. The differences on the Russian side are apt to find involuntary expression in such extreme manifestations as the Stalin dictatorship; but they include also aspects of no less extreme nobility. No appreciation of the enemy, of the strength and vulnerability of the Stalin régime, that is to say, can be of any use unless this régime is related to the people who have made it possible. It is because of this that so many books offering an indictment of the Stalin régime in terms intelligible to Western understanding, books like Kravchenko's *I Chose Freedom* and Koestler's *The Yogi and the Commissar,* have done almost certainly more harm than good. They tell nothing but the truth, but they leave out Russia.

One of the chief reasons for our confusion in the present conflict is, as one would expect, ignorance. But it is not the sort of ignorance that can be set right by a visit to Russia to see it for oneself and get to know the people. It goes a great deal deeper than that. The particular aspects of it which matter most in our present context are those to do with the Russian attitude to life in general and to society and government in particular. Our ignorance here is aggravated by the very human habit of thinking about other nations in terms of their institutions, instead of thinking about the institutions in terms of the people who evolved them. Parallel with this, and in spite of continual demonstrations to the contrary, is our persistent belief that the same word, or its literal equivalent, means the same thing in all countries. Where Russia is concerned this double error works with quite exceptional potency, because, for one reason and another, most of us do not know the Russian people at all. So we are forced to think of them in terms of their institutions, and we are forced to think of their institutions in terms of our own. Nothing could be more fatal. It is not only a matter of abstract words, like "democracy" and "freedom," and it is not enough to say, when we discover that democracy means something quite different on the lips of Mr. Vishinsky from what it means on the lips of Mr. Warren Austin, that the Russian is deliberately corrupting that word. Sometimes he is; sometimes he is not.

But the point I am trying to make is that simple concrete words may be as productive of cross-purposes as abstract concepts. To the British soldier the word "transport" calls up an image of a phalanx of three-ton trucks, solid, immaculate, and uniform. But pronounce that word

to a Russian and he will see in his mind's eye a long and
straggling procession of farm carts hauled by thin and
hairy ponies; and even the farm cart is a flimsy affair, like
a large wooden pig trough on extemporized wheels. During the period of the first Five-Year Plans the word
"wrecker" caused us a great deal of concern. But we
should have reflected that at that time the average Russian
factory was not what we should call a factory at all, but a
sort of improvised workshop. Even the new and shining
modern production lines were staffed mainly by the sort
of people who, in Great Britain, would never have been
allowed within reach of a machine. The atmosphere was
the sort of atmosphere most easily achieved by populating
a machine shop with peasant characters from Chekhov,
Turgenev, or Tolstoi. Parts got lost, machines were not
bedded down and threw themselves over when they were
started up, whole batteries of machines would stand idle
for months for lack of simple maintenance (as they do in
fact to this day), cars would be put together without distributors because the supply of distributors had been exhausted and production must not stop. And the only way
to bring this kind of thing to an end was to call it sabo-
tage, or wrecking, and punish it with the most fearful
severity. Indeed, it was wrecking. The sort of carelessness
which the ordinary Russian would dismiss with a shrug
would be known in the West as criminal negligence. And
the fact that charges of wrecking were impartially levelled
at any individual whom the party or the police wanted to
put away did not in the least alter the fact that criminal
negligence, or wrecking, arising from the fecklessness and
idleness of the Russian peasant let loose in the factories,
was no less real, and a great deal more common, than sabo-
tage for political motives. The Soviet government attributed political motives to all criminal negligence,

partly because in Russia the political offence, the offence against the state or communal property, has always been regarded as more serious than the crime against the individual, such as murder, and partly to make the people more politically conscious in the Russian manner.

Faced with the accumulated evidence of the harshness and cruelty of life in the Soviet Union, but having nothing against the Russian people as such, we are inclined to attribute the things we dislike to the régime of the moment. Rarely does anyone ask whether there may not be something inherently Russian in the evils which today we put down to the Kremlin, but which only the day before yesterday we visited on the tsars. Even more rarely does anyone ask whether, in Russian eyes, what seem to us the worst iniquities appear as iniquities at all. These seem very obvious questions to ask. I suppose the reason we so rarely think of asking them is that, for example, to us, it is all but inconceivable that any nation, any set of people under the sun, could fail to regard our own conception of individual liberty as the ultimate summit of human felicity. This, I think, is where we go wrong.

Where the Russians are concerned it is particularly easy to go wrong in this way. We know by their writings of the nineteenth century that they possess extreme independence of mind and spirit. We know that they are peculiarly open-minded and susceptible to influences of every kind. We know, further, that the history of Russia flickers with peasant risings, great and small. We know that the peasants, as serfs, were used harshly, kept down, and deprived of all human rights. We know that the revolutionary spirits among the Russian intelligentsia cried out against this oppression and were sent into exile for it. And knowing all this, knowing also that in the end the tsars were swept away by a successful revolution, we very naturally conclude that what the Russian people cried out against and finally drowned in blood was what we ourselves in their position would have cried out against: namely, the autocratic principle and all its works. But I think this conclusion is wrong. The Russian people did not rise up against any principle at all. They rose up, as they had done many times before, against intolerable conditions of life; but their violence was not directed against the autocracy as such. It was certainly not directed against the tsardom. The people who wanted to get rid of the Tsar were the new commercial magnates who found themselves held back by him. As far as the people were concerned, their fury was directed against a corrupt bureaucracy and an effete nobility which were making life too hard for them. They wanted an alleviation of the conditions of their lives, not the overthrow of a political principle.

The stock reply to questions about most Russian anomalies is that they are a backward people. But why are they so backward? Their country is large and rich—the largest and richest in the world. Why have they failed to develop this country, which, in the eighteenth century, was certainly a great deal less backward than North America at that time. The answer to that, of course, again the stock answer, is that Russia was ruled by an autocrat through a corrupt bureaucracy, and that until 1861 the mass of her people were serfs, or bondslaves. All that is true; but what does it explain? Why was Russia ruled by an autocrat? Why was her bureaucracy corrupt? Why was her nobility effete? Why were nine-tenths of her people serfs—and far more slave-like in the year 1800 than in the year 1600? Why, when the rest of Europe was flinging off the last traces of the feudal system, was Russia hugging it more closely round her than ever before? Is it true to say that all this was the cause of Russia's backwardness? Might it

not be more true to say that it was the result of her backwardness? Then, if so, again why was she backward? And,
in any case, what do we mean by backwardness?

These questions, and others like them, come pouring
out the moment one starts to contemplate with an open
mind, with a mind as free as can be from Western assumptions, either the history of Russia or the contemporary
Soviet way of life, which are inseparable. We cannot possibly answer them here in detail. But it is a good thing to
ask them and then let the mind work on them, because
they are the very questions which, sooner or later, one will
find oneself asking if one speculates long enough and
logically enough about the behaviour of Messrs. Molotov,
Vishinsky, and Malik. They are not rhetorical questions.
By answering them we should find the answer to our first
question: what is the fundamental difference between the
Russian and Western European attitudes towards life and
society? The questions demand answers, because it is impossible to pretend that in the days before the machine
gun a great nation of peasant serfs, scattered over the biggest land mass in the world, could be kept down by a
supreme autocrat working through a corrupt bureaucracy
and an indolent nobility—unless in some way the peasants
connived at being kept down. No autocrat could have held
down the British people in a state of increasing bondage.
The English would not have put up with it. The conclusion is that the Russian people did put up with it; and it
is worth bearing in mind that when serfdom was finally
abolished in 1861, this action was not a surrender to a
popular movement (the serfs did little or nothing to free
themselves). Their liberation came about, for one reason
and another, by the usual ukase from above. In 1805 a
Russian tsar had opposed the notion of putting the serfs
into a distinctive dress "because they will recognize each

other and realize how many they are." There were then thirty-five million serfs out of a population of forty-six millions. But when the liberation came there were petitions from the serfs against it. "We are yours," they would say, "but the land is ours. Let us go on as we are."

There were, of course, popular movements. Russian history is full of them, and the most celebrated, the Stenka Razin rebellion in the seventeenth century and the Pugachev rebellion in the eighteenth, were initially successful. But they soon flickered out ignominiously, because they lacked an idea, or faith. They had no more significance than the innumerable burnings of local manor houses by infuriated villagers. They were despairing revolts on the part of the oppressed people who could stand their immediate miseries no longer, which is a very different thing from a political revolt. Indeed, the rising which overthrew the Romanovs and paved the way for the present régime was not very different in kind, except that this time it was stimulated by businessmen and reforming nobles. It had no real idea, as far as the masses were concerned. The idea was provided eight months later by Lenin, whose October Revolution was a political revolution with a faith, which was staged within the framework of a typical Russian revolt with no more significance than the stampeding of cattle driven crazy by the warble fly.

Elsewhere I have tried to suggest why this should be; but for our immediate purpose we have to decide what the Russians are, not how they became what they are. It is enough for the moment to say that the society developed in Tsarist Russia was an autocracy based on serfdom, and that the serfs, although they grumbled bitterly, although they detested the government and everything to do with it, although they considered it their first duty to cheat the government on every possible occasion (and in so doing, incidentally, developed a mode of double-talk, which the present régime has taken over from them and developed exceedingly), still regarded the tsar as above the government and all humanity. Not only did they take no stock in that idea of individual freedom which we regard as the *sine qua non* of existence, but they would almost certainly have despised it had it been offered to them. These people were the immediate forebears, often the grandfathers, sometimes the fathers, of the great mass of the people of Russia today, including several members of the highest councils of the Kremlin.

We have, as I have said, to ask why. We have also to ask how this attitude—we could call it nonpolitical, but that would beg the question; we could call it servile, but that would not be true—is to be reconciled with the known facts about Russian independence of mind, Russian boldness of spirit, Russian resistance to being governed, Russian hankering after anarchy. Indeed, if we can suggest the secret of this reconciliation, which must be effected in the bosom of every Russian simply by the fact of his being a Russian, then I think we shall have suggested a working answer to the "Why?" And the keyword, I believe, occurs in that last phrase: "the Russian hankering after anarchy." For anarchy is an absolute: it is the absolute of freedom; and the Russian is an absolutist. If he cannot have anarchy, which is absolute freedom, it does not matter what he has. And he cannot have anarchy: the Russian knows that as well as we do. So he washes his hands of the whole business of freedom and has an autocracy instead. We, not being absolutists by temperament, take the nearest thing to absolute freedom we can get, which varies with social conditions from age to age. We call this compromise, or *savoir vivre,* or common sense, or a sense of proportion. A Russian would call it betrayal—betrayal of self.

That, it goes without saying, is an oversimplification; but I believe it takes us very close to the heart of the Russian nature, which I have seen explained in no other way. There are two hard facts which appear to be contradictory, which are indeed contradictory, but which nevertheless exist together: independence to the point of anarchy and an easy acceptance of autocracy. In the Time of the Troubles in the early seventeenth century, when the Poles had occupied Moscow and offered union to the Muscovite boyars, they promised also freedom from the tyranny of an autocratic tsar. But the boyars replied in their gloomy forest stiffness, in the accents of Mr. Molotov rejecting temptation, that the Polish idea of freedom looked to them more like licence, and that, in any case, rather than live in a society where brother might be exalted above brother, they preferred to submit as equals to the will of a supreme overlord: "If the tsar acts unjustly, it is his will. It is better to suffer injury from the tsar than from one's brother. For he is the common ruler of us all." This was not very long after the boyars themselves had suffered so bloodily at the hands of Ivan the Terrible, a perfect reversal of the situation between King John of England and his barons at Runnymede two centuries earlier. They knew what autocracy could do. But they preferred it, and, when the Poles had been chased away, put up the Romanovs to rule them. Or, again, to return to the peasants: when Pugachev raised the peasantry in the early years of Catherine the Great, he was able to do this only by pretending to be the dead Tsar Peter, returned from exile to fight for his own and the rights of the people of Russia against the landowners. One could multiply these interesting examples, but it will be enough if I quote the words of Leontiev: "Sometimes I dream that a Russian tsar may put himself at the head of the Socialist movement and organize it, as Constantine organized Christianity."

The Russians are also receptive. They are receptive to every foreign influence. The Russian nation is a group of people each member of which is unshakably convinced that he is as good as anyone else, and who is equally convinced that everyone else is as good as he is; who regards it as a degradation of the lowest kind to see the liberty of action of one man curtailed in any way for the benefit of another; who believes, above all, that it is the prime duty of man to be true to himself, at least in his heart; who regards compromise not as a sign of strength but as a sign of the dilution of personality, or self-betrayal; who is, moreover, susceptible in the extreme to outside influences of every kind; who is, in a word, experimental in temperament and mentally free, in the way that, in the West, only the artist is experimental and free. When you have a group composed of such members, who, nevertheless, faced with a cruel and hostile universe, realize the necessity for combination in a coherent community and yet refuse to recognize any hierarchy among themselves, then, evidently, without a very tight and universally acknowledged control from above, there is going to be an immediate state of anarchy. But the Russians know too much about life to believe that a nation can exist in a state of anarchy, however much they may desire that consummation. So they accept, as a necessary evil, the tight control from above. Hence the tsarist autocracy. Hence the Kremlin dictatorship. Hence, too, the passion for orthodoxy, any orthodoxy which, imposed from above and, as it were, outside the community, will keep the people together: first the Greek Church, with its accent on ritual; now the Communist Party, with its rigid body of doctrine. Hence, too, the formalism of so many Russian institutions. Hence, finally, the interminable protocols of Messrs. Molotov and Vishinsky. All this, I suggest, is the rigidity of a naturally too fluid people who have to forge round themselves hoops of iron or disintegrate entirely.

It all seems to come from a natural individualism which makes our own vaunted individualism look like an abandonment of personality. So, indeed, it is; because every single institution in Great Britain, as well as America, depends for its smooth running on the voluntary adaptation of extreme points of view—in a world of personal points of view—to other points of view. This the Russian will not have. He would rather be coerced by a supreme and untouchable authority than dilute his individuality in the least degree or surrender his claim to equality with all men by voluntary participation in what we should call a democratic society based on mutual give-and-take. It is all take with him, or all give; it is all domination, or all submission. So he submits. This has gone on for a long time. In the ancient commune, or even the mediæval free city, he contrived an equalitarian society run by a freely elected elder, who, during his term of office, was a dictator; while when it came to the larger organizations of society, such as the whole nation, he could still regard all men as equal under God and the tsar. He rendered certain things to God and certain things to the tsar. It might be everything he had. But, essentially, it was submission under protest to *force majeure,* and the great thing was that he kept his soul. He made no concessions to what he did not believe. We, on the other hand, with our perpetual concessions, with our whole existence based on concessions, would appear to him to have made a bargain with the devil. "The Russians," said Professor Miliukov, "lack the cement of hypocrisy." And this, I think, is what he meant. It is one

way of putting it. Another is to say that they lack the sense
of compromise, of give-and-take. Lacking this, they have
to be held together, or down, by an autocratic pressure.
There is something to be said for this sort of arrangement.
The trouble is that it ignores the effect of absolute power
both on the wielders of that power and on those who submit to it.

Granted this much, it is clearly nonsense to suggest that
Russia is a backward country because for so long its people
were held down by an absolutist tyranny. It is also nonsense to see in Lenin's victory an arbitrary bolt from the
blue, having no connection with the nature of Russia. For
this is part of the background against which we must see
the Soviet régime. It does not mean that the people will
always put up with it: they overthrew the tsars, and, as we
shall later see, for large numbers of them the present
régime has gone too far. But it is enough to show the
danger of reading our own experience and feelings into
the Russian people. No matter how deeply the Russian
people as a whole may abhor certain aspects of the present
régime, they have, to put it crudely, asked for it. Further,
the aspects of it which they most deplore are by no means
necessarily the aspects which we in the West most deplore.
And, finally, the quality of their dislike of the régime is in
many ways different from the quality of our long-range
dislike of it.

To take an example. Most Russians dislike the secret
police on principle. But their dislike does not amount to
horror at the very idea of a secret police. They dislike it
in much the same way as we, in England, dislike the income tax—as, that is to say, a lamentable but necessary
evil. They find it hard, if not impossible, to conceive of
a society without a secret police; and they are only outraged when the police overstep themselves even by Rus-

sian standards. On the other hand, the collectivization of small holdings, which to us might seem to be quite a good idea, was resisted by the Russian peasant with a bitterness of feeling which we should reserve for the worst excesses of a licentious tyranny.

6

The Expansionist Tradition

THE STRANGE ABSOLUTISM of the Russian temperament, on which we have touched, the absence of any instinct for compromise, or of what we call a sense of proportion, or common sense, leads naturally to a state of mind in which there are only two possible patterns of behaviour: total submission or total domination. Mr. Geoffrey Gorer makes this point with extreme elaboration in his fascinating analysis of the character of the Great Russians: he traces it, in the style of the Freudian anthropologist, to the Russian habit of swaddling babies, and all that springs therefrom. Not being a trained anthropologist I would be inclined to attribute the Russian habit of swaddling babies to ingrained characteristics derived from other causes. But be that as it may, the habit of mind is there; and it has a very direct bearing on one aspect of our current problem: the nature of Russian expansionism. This, like the duplicity of Russian statesmen, is something different in kind from the expansionism of other nations.

Russia has been an expanding power since the foundation of the Muscovite state in the fourteenth century. The First World War and the revolution gave her a setback; but Stalin has already made good the losses of the old empire, with one or two small and provisional exceptions, such as Finland, and has added something of his own, so that the Soviet Empire is now larger than the Tsarist Empire ever was. The Soviet Union also wields an influence beyond her borders far greater than that wielded by the tsars. The tsars, moreover, were hemmed in by great powers: Prussia, Austria, and Japan. Stalin is not.

But to say that Russia is traditionally an expanding power is not at all to say that she is a warlike power; and this is a point of the first importance. For here is another of our contemporary confusions: misreading, perhaps, the lessons taught by Germany and Mussolini's Italy, we have come to identify expansionist politics with a warlike spirit. One of the many Russian paradoxes is that the most expansionist power in the world is also one of the least belligerent powers in the world. This is not because Russia has, or ever has had, any moral scruples about going to war: she has none at all. It is simply because she does not like going to war.

In the simplest terms, the traditional Russian expansionist drive can be broken down into three aspects: the strategic; the economic; and the missionary, or messianic, aspect. All these existed long before the revolution, coming into being in that order. They are now complicated by a fourth aspect, the world revolutionary aspect. This, on the face of it, is something quite new; but actually we shall see that it is simply one manifestation of the messianic aspect.

The strategic aspect of Russian expansionism is easy to grasp, although at first sight it may seem difficult to understand why a power which controls more territory than any other in the world, and with a population incapable of filling it and developing it, should still hanker after more. This query rests on a false assumption: that Russia has always been a state of vast dimensions; whereas, in fact, six hundred years ago it was very small indeed. The occupation of the great Eurasian land mass, from the Bug to the Pacific, from the Arctic Ocean to the Caspian, was completed only recently. The Russian state, which is the heir to the princedom of Muscovy, started life very modestly with a limited and extremely vulnerable territory round and about the headwaters of the Volga. Born in self-defence against the occupying Tartars, in order to succeed at all it had to keep up a ceaseless outward pressure, first swallowing up the rival Russian princedoms, then rising against the Golden Horde, which had held the Russians in subjection for two hundred and fifty years, then pushing back the encroaching peoples of the west and the south: the Swedes, the Lithuanians, the Teutonic Knights, the Poles, the Turks.

The theatre of operations was an interminable plain with no natural boundaries against invasion. It had to be filled up; and in this long process was born the peculiar Russian method of defence by attack. It could be said that the very spirit of the old Russia was expansion. The Russians voyaged across the plain, much as Tudor seamen explored the oceans. It was hard to know where to stop. If the Muscovites themselves had not expanded outwards from their centre and deep into the plain, their neighbours would have done so in their place. And for ever afterwards the plain was to prove a source of danger—up to our own days when the German armour overran the western levels. The problem permanently facing the Russians was very much like the problem which faced the

Eighth Army in the western desert: Benghazi could not be held without command of the desert for a thousand miles on either side. In the last resort, to secure Cairo, you had to hold Tripoli and all the land between. So the Russians went to Vladivostok, to Samarkand, to Kamchatka, to the White Sea and the Baltic, to the Caucasus and the Crimea. And this habit, at one time stark necessity, became, as it were, part of an unconscious principle of life. Russia forgot how to stop. She even expanded across the Bering Strait into Alaska before she realized quite what she had done. And then, thinking better of it, and suddenly realizing that the only way to hold Alaska was to continue her expansion across the whole North American continent, she sold Alaska and withdrew across the water.

Expansion westwards was less successful. In this direction Russia was opposed by the organized resistance of superior cultures. And so, in due course, she stopped. In face of organized resistance the Russians have always stopped. It is not simply that they are afraid to fight. The sudden impact of a strong wall seems to have the effect of waking them up and making them look where they are going. It is as though they walked in their sleep. What seems to happen is that their expansion is carried out in obedience to a simple law, which they never think of questioning until it leads them into trouble. It is a natural habit of indefinite growth along the line of least resistance, arising from an enforced preoccupation with security which, through the centuries, has become an obsession.

In fact, the sleepwalking image has a certain aptness. As we shall see in a moment, Russian expansion has taken place almost in spite of the Russians and in face of a profound impulse towards contraction. So marked has this conflict been at times that it is scarcely an exaggeration to say that when a particular expansionist thrust has been frustrated the Russians have recoiled and sunk down into passivity, almost with a sigh of relief. Total resignation replaces total arrogance.

The economic aspect of Russian expansionism is more commonplace in its origins and motives. In the past it has meant the securing of access to the sea; more lately it has meant the securing of certain maritime outlets, plus the harnessing to the Russian economy of certain resources situated outside Russia. The question of access to the sea and the securing of these outlets when once gained may seem irrelevant today; but it is relevant enough, since it was the behaviour of the tsars when engaged in securing these objectives, above all the freedom of the Black Sea and its outlet, the Dardanelles, which not only gave rise to the image of Russia as a looming threat to the Western world, but also provided a training ground for the special Russian diplomatic technique.

The third aspect of traditional Russian expansionism is the missionary, or messianic, aspect; and it abounds in contradictions. Through the centuries Imperial Russia developed a quasi-mystical sense of moral superiority, and with it, later, a sense of mission. It dates back to the days when Russia was shut off from the West by a barrier hardly less effective than the iron curtain which today the Soviet Union has lowered in face of the West. While Western Europe was developing a new civilization after its emergence from the Middle Ages, the Russians were cut off from the new spirit by the occupying Tartars and by the barrier put up against the Tartars by the western neighbours of Muscovy. When the Tartars were at last overthrown, in 1482, the Russians found that they and their western neighbours had been developing for a long time on very different lines. The differences were symbolized by the difference in religion: Russian Christianity,

coming from Byzantium, was spurned by the Catholic
West.

At first the Russians, instead of trying to break this barrier down, gloried in their apartness and exclusiveness,
which fitted perfectly the new conception of Moscow as
the Third Rome, which grew up when Constantinople fell
to the Turks, leaving, in Russian eyes, Moscow as the true
heir to the Christian leadership and the only repository of
the true Christian faith.

I have already spoken of the profound impulse towards
contraction round the inviolable centre which is the
counterweight to the expansionist dynamic of the Russians; and it is here that the duality has its core. The
messianic tendency may express itself in one of two ways,
diametrically opposed; and the conflict between these two
opposing impulses was the chief factor in Russian policy
from the end of the fifteenth century to the outbreak of
the First World War. So deeply rooted a conflict is not on
the face of it likely to be exorcised by a simple act of
revolution; and in fact it persists to this day and may yet
bring about changes in Soviet policy which will appear
unaccountable unless we know something of their origin.
Already quite remarkable changes have occurred during
the past fifteen years, as we shall see, although these have
been masked by the momentum of the revolutionary idea.

It will be convenient to call these opposing impulses,
which in practice amount to opposing traditions (it is incorrect to speak of the Russian tradition: there are two
quite distinct traditions), the Muscovite and the Petrine
tradition. This is an oversimplification because, as one
would expect, there being no purity in this world, the two
are frequently mixed; but it will do.

The Muscovite tradition may be defined as an impulse
of withdrawal from the outside world, above all from

contamination by what the Russian in his heart must call
the Eternal West, as we should speak of the Eternal East.
As we have seen, instead of striving to catch up with the
Renaissance culture, with its emphasis on the individual,
which was beginning to flower in Western Europe at the
very moment when the Russians got rid of the Tartars and
could turn their eyes westwards, they sank, as it were, back
into themselves and gloried in their own apartness. It is
quite fair to speak of "catching up," because three hundred years earlier the Russians of the principality of Kiev
(which later lost the day to Moscow) were very much a
part of the main stream of European culture, obtaining
their rulers and their aristocracy from the Scandinavian
Vikings, as the English likewise did, and trafficking freely
down the waterways with Byzantium, Greece, and the
valley of the Danube. The Tartars from the East put a
stop to all that; Moscow swallowed Kiev; and when the
time came for Moscow to join Europe once more it preferred to sulk and make a virtue of its own backwardness,
repelling the culture of the West as something corrupt
and frivolous and false. Corruption, to the Russian, means
essentially the surrender of the soul to alien forces, while
falsity is the pretence that things are better than they are.
In a word, although the Muscovites realized their own ineptitude in face of life, and that we, in the West, had made
a more workmanlike job of it, they were by no means inclined to agree that the workmanlike approach to life was
valid, having a profound conviction that life was a good
deal deeper and harsher and more complex than we in the
West pretend. To them our Renaissance civilization with
its neat and practical categories, its worship of commerce,
was altogether too easy and slick, too good to be true; and
it appeared to them that for the sake of a quiet and tidy
existence, for the sake of "making something out of life,"

as we say, we had committed the unforgivable sin of agree-
ing to pretend that life was other than it was, that the
overpowering mysteries of existence, of which the Russian
is ever conscious (hence his convulsive efforts to find some
all-embracing orthodoxy, or simplification, for the comfort
of which he will submit to the heaviest pressures on his
individual will), do not really exist. The underlying idea
is that for our own convenience we have betrayed our true
selves. In a word, we compromise with evil and wish it out
of existence; but the evil remains, contaminating all we
touch. The Russian will not compromise with evil. Evil
exists, he will say. It cannot be denied. It can only be opposed by good—the absolute of evil opposed by the absolute of good. Where evil is too strong, then it must be
acknowledged and the knee bent in submission. Render
unto Lucifer the things that are Lucifer's. Do not delude
yourselves by feeble attempts at palliation or at disguising
the terrible truth. And so we find the eternal dualism of
Russian art symbolized in the saintly fool and the evil
genius. And in Russian life one and the same man, let
him be, for the sake of topicality, an intelligent official of
the M.V.D., can combine in himself aspects of extreme
goodness and extreme evil. Or we find a nineteenth-
century liberal Russian thinker, Alexander Herzen, re-
coiling from the crass barbarities of the tsarist régime and,
sheltered by the enlightened governments of Western
Europe, himself turning bitterly on the West, which
prided itself on its liberality:

> We share your doubts, but your faith does not cheer
> us. We share your hatred, but we do not understand
> your devotion to what your forefathers have bequeathed
> you; we are too downtrodden, too unhappy, to be satis-
> fied with your half-measures. You are restrained by

scruples, you are held back by second thoughts. We have neither second thoughts nor scruples; all we lack is strength. . . .

The distinction between your laws and our imperial decrees is confined to the formula with which they begin. Our imperial decrees begin with the crushing truth: "The tsar has been pleased to command"; your laws begin with a revolting falsehood, the ironical abuse of the name of the French people, and the words Liberty, Equality, Fraternity. The code of Nicholas is drawn up for the benefit of the Autocracy to the detriment of its subjects. The Napoleonic code has exactly the same character. We are held by too many chains to fasten fresh ones about us of our own free will. In this respect we stand precisely on a level with our peasants. We submit to brute force. We are slaves because we have no possibility of being free; but we accept nothing from our foes.

The immediate Western retort to that sort of thing is: "Stuff and nonsense! What you want is a nice brisk walk." And that is fair enough. So is Miss Macaulay's sharp, good-humouredly contemptuous remark that the Russian sees things as they are, and proceeds to make them a good deal worse. On the other hand, the attitude is the product of a burning, defiant, *useless* integrity, of a kind which, however wrongheaded its conclusions, the world badly needs. Along with infinite corruption, it still exists in Soviet Russia, and it may yet save us from our own worst materialist excesses.

Until the Romanovs came and Peter the Great built his window on to Europe, cut off the beards of his nobles, and propelled them from their stuffy wooden hives into the vast Italianate chambers of his new city on the Neva, the

tradition of withdrawal from contamination by the outside world was very much in the ascendant. Periodically
there were intellectual raids on the West, notably under
Ivan the Terrible, to find alliances, to find architects, to
profit by the latest technical discoveries; but these were
the exception. The rule was a mood of atavistic, inward-
turning sullenness, heightened by self-distrust. And, indeed, even after Peter had tried to change all that, reaction and isolationism would succeed as night follows day
the vigorous and brutal plunges towards a Western orientation. Only in the nineteenth century did the St. Petersburg tradition finally conquer. And now, instead of saving
the world by turning away from it and preserving the Russian spirit from pollution, the profound messianic impulse
found a new expression: the saving of the world by Russian might.

I am not in the least suggesting that the St. Petersburg
expansionism, which reached its peak in the nineteenth
century, was entirely a missionary affair. The strategic and
economic motives, which we have already considered, were
probably uppermost in the minds of the ministers responsible—above all, the habit of expansion along the line of
least resistance coupled with the all-or-nothing spirit of
the absolutist temperament. But its peculiar quality, dif-
ferentiating it from the imperial pretensions manifested
in all the great powers at that epoch, was undoubtedly due
to a sense of the divine right of the Russians to rule, which
was now extended to cover the mission of Slavdom as a
whole. Thus it was that, during the imperial fever, the
Russians found a convenient pretext for their own ambitions for westward expansion in the legend of the united
Slavs. And the practical projection of hitherto vague and
generalized aspirations was the assumption by the tsar of

the rôle of protector, not only of all Slavs everywhere, but also of all Christians under Turkish rule throughout the Middle East and the Balkans. Thus, to take a single example, the Eastern Question, which bedevilled Europe from the moment when Catherine appeared on the Black Sea, offers a classic practical example of the way in which all three expansionist impulses in practice worked together. The strategic impulse of expansion along the line of least resistance, dictated by an obsession with security, found expression in the persistent attempt to push the Western powers out of the Black Sea by denying them access to the Straits—an action which the West (i.e., Britain and France) interpreted as an attempt by the Russians to achieve a naval deployment in the Mediterranean. The economic impulse centred on the Black Sea coast itself, which, in Odessa, provided a warm-water port which could be used all the year round; but Odessa could be bottled up, or even raided and destroyed, by any power having access to the Black Sea through the Straits. The messianic impulse was reflected in the Russian attitude towards the dismemberment of Turkey, "the sick man of Europe," which still managed to tyrannize over the Slavs and Christians inhabiting Turkey's Balkan possessions.

There was also the hatred of England, which, towards the end of the Romanov dynasty, became a motive in its own right. Hatred of England had been responsible for the one downright aggressive project in Russian history, when the mad Tsar Paul, infuriated by English pretensions in the Middle East, plotted with Napoleon a crackbrained and abortive expedition to conquer India. But it was in the Far East that Russian actions were almost invariably conditioned by the bogey of England.

England then, as America today, was seen as the Coca-

Cola culture; that is to say, she lived by trade and, when she thought at all, saw in uninhibited commerce the redemption of the world. And just as today the dedicated opponents of the Coca-Cola culture are the Russians, so it was a hundred years ago. We have already commented upon the Russian contempt for the shopkeeping habits of the English, which had been obtruded on Muscovy from the days of Ivan the Terrible, when the first English embassies affronted that sultry autocrat by showing no interest in anything at all but trade: "We knowe that merchants' matters are to bee heard," admitted Ivan in one of his expansive conversations with Elizabeth's trusted envoy, "for that they are the stay of our princely treasures; but first the princes' affairs are to be established and then merchants'." And he could not conceive of a prince worthy of the name who considered the affairs of his merchants as more important than his own dignity. Time and time again in the nineteenth century we find Russian statesmen fulminating against British imperialism with its emphasis on commerce. Their own imperialism, as already remarked, was rooted in an impatient conviction of the nobility of the Russian destiny. At its crudest this found expression in the jingo press of St. Petersburg, which, two years before the First World War, which saw the end of Imperial Russia (and only seven years after the Russo-Japanese war, which had seen its deepest shame), could write in terms like these:

> Our time-honoured policy, from the days of the Varangians down to the reign of Alexander III, was founded on the axiom that Russia must expand territorially at the expense of her neighbours. In spite of her thousand years of existence, Russia is still on the road towards her national and political frontiers.

But the mystique of Russian expansion and Russian destiny was by no means confined to professional journalists and politicians. Dostoevski was full of it. Herzen whom we have already cited, was full of it. Muraviev himself, the most fascinating and dynamic personality in the history of Sino-Russian relations, combined in himself, as only a Russian could do, all the features of a romantic revolutionary with all the features of an empire builder and a statesman. The difference between Muraviev and Cecil Rhodes is the difference between Russia and England. Muraviev detested England and was determined to save the Far East, by Russian might, from English commercial exploitation. His cast of mind is well displayed by the juxtaposition of two facts. In one breath he planned for a grand federation of Russia and America, which would redeem the world from the stale trivialities of Western European civilization; and in the next breath he would be expressing the pathological suspicions of the Russian diplomat about the smallest details of British behaviour. Two Englishmen, an explorer and a geologist, travelling in Eastern Siberia in 1848, aroused his most agonized fears, and the future of the world, conceived in grandiose terms, seemed to him to hang upon their actions. "If they sail down the Amur River," he announced, "British ships will occupy Sakhalin next spring." On top of that, while a fervent servant of his government, he contrived to be the friend of Kropotkin and the patron of Bakunin, with whom he would discuss, in the intervals of worrying himself to death about the significance of solitary British travellers, who must certainly be spies, the rearrangement of the universe upon a cosmic scale, starting modestly with the Russo-American federation.

If we seem to have wandered far from our subject, I don't think, in fact, we have. Soviet Russia has the same strategic and economic preoccupations as Imperial Russia. The minds of the Soviet leaders, with the exception of Stalin himself, are Russian minds. And the Bolsheviks are also interested in the redemption of the world. At first they wanted to save the world by Marxism. But now . . .?

2. *Stalinism*

1

The Politburo

THIRTY MILES to the west of Moscow, a little off the great military highway running through Mozhaisk to Smolensk, there is a patch of enchanting country. Here the Moskva River winds through little wooded hills; and the sunken lanes, shadowed with sycamore and chestnut, have quite an English look.

Driving aimlessly through these lanes (as until quite recently you could, even in Stalin's Russia, provided you had access to a car and could speak enough Russian to get the chauffeur off the main roads), you are suddenly disturbed by a note of incongruity: clustered round a sign-post at a minor crossroads are half a dozen policemen, all in their best uniforms, with tommy guns under their arms. They are special police, not the ordinary beat-pounding militia with dark-blue bands round their caps, but members of Mr. Kruglov's M.V.D., the latest transformation of the Cheka, G.P.U., N.K.V.D. They have light-blue bands round their hats and live extremely well. A little disconcerted, but in no way impeded, you proceed, recalling apprehensively that somewhere in this general direction Stalin and his lieutenants are said to repair for country delights.

At the next crossroads there are twice six policemen, including some with rifles and fixed bayonets, the long, spiky Russian bayonet, round in section. But beyond a hard look they take no notice. And then the nervous impression that you have got into somebody's private grounds is dizzily augmented, for over the next two miles you find yourself cruising like a royal procession between two extended lines of police, all armed to the teeth and flattened into the steep banks on either side of the lane, one every twenty yards or so. But still nothing happens—though, you cannot help thinking, something very well might, if you stopped to look over a stile. There is nothing for it but to go forward. . . . Until, quite suddenly, the lane has widened, and slap across it, barring all further progress, tower the biggest iron gates in the world. There is nothing to do but go back.

Even as your engine stalls, you find yourself surrounded. Behind you is half a company of police (these M.V.D. men are trained, organized, and armed like a crack military formation, though they are never used to fight a war), while from haystacks and little huts by the iron gates the other half-company emerges. But only to look. Not a word is spoken. And in that moment you become aware of a side lane, skirting away round a tall fence, made of sheet iron, which comes right up to the gateway. In the silence you are aware of bird song; and somehow the whole weight of the vast, impersonal plain leading all the way to Siberia seems to make itself felt through that delusive boskage, fragrant in the sunshine of spring. There is still not a sound from the M.V.D. as your driver restarts the car, backs it a little, swings it round into the escape road, hoping to goodness it leads somewhere. Without a word, and with a mixed armament at the ready, the lifeguards watch your stuttering departure. . . .

You have been as near as you will ever get to Stalin, unless you are somebody's special envoy; and it is a good deal closer than most foreigners would believe you could get. You have stalled your engine at the very spot where the great bulletproof Packard, or Zis, with the blue glass and the often-drawn blinds, finishes its journey from the midnight Kremlin. You have listened, a little abstractedly, it is true, to the song of Stalin's chaffinches.

On the way back, round the loop to the main road, there are more police. The iron fence flanks the road on one side for a mile or more, and then curves away through trees. Here and there you pass lesser gates with lesser guards. Then, out in the open country, you drive through a village which looks like a military camp: police in undress are all over the place, playing cards in their shirt-sleeves on the village green; cleaning guns on doorsteps; drilling, with shining leatherwork, on the side of the road; examining the bowels of motorcars; carrying water buckets from the village pump. Then two or three more villages, model villages, bright with new paint, spick and span and filled with smiling inhabitants—model inhabitants, you might say, personally chosen by Mr. Kruglov and given a special paint allowance. Potemkin villages, only permanent, unlike the temporary exhibitions run up by Catherine's favourite to please her Imperial Majesty on her journeys—Potemkin villages designed to impress Stalin with the fairness and prosperity of his vast dominions on the rare occasions when he motors to the Kremlin by daylight—seeing, through those armoured glass windows, one imagines, a landscape all in blue.

More policemen at the junction with the main road; then the long swoop down the best highway in Russia, meeting more police on motor bikes; then the approaches to Moscow, lined by the best blocks of workers' flats in Moscow, inhabited by workers of a very special kind; and into the crowded city, where you turn off. But if you were in Stalin's Zis, or Packard, you would tear down the Arbat, miraculously cleared, across the traffic without a single check, and, with guards ready at attention and a thin little bell shrilling in the red brick tower, still at speed through the narrow archway—to safety at last behind the Kremlin walls. And so it is, not only with Stalin, but with all the members of the supreme government of the U.S.S.R., the Politburo, whose country villas lie concealed behind those lesser gates with lesser guards. The interesting thing is that there is nothing about them in the constitution.

The constitutional government of the U.S.S.R. is the Supreme Soviet, which is a popularly elected body, a two-chamber affair of delegates from all over the Union, who may or may not be important Communists. Elected every four years, by the single list technique, with 99 per cent unanimity, they meet twice a year, for ten days at a time, in a very fine hall inside the Kremlin—not a debating chamber, but an auditorium, to ratify the legislation en-acted in their absence by their Presidium. The chairman of this Presidium, now the ex-trade-union leader, Shver-nik, is the titular head of the state, or president, whose functions include pinning medals on their recipients and exchanging birthday greetings and other compliments with the heads of other states.

One of the main responsibilities of the Presidium is to appoint the ministers who run the departmental work of government. Until 1948 these ministers were called Peo-ple's Commissars. There are now over fifty of them, for

the number of government departments in a land where
every activity is state-controlled must necessarily be very
large. Together they form the Council of Ministers, and
they are nominally responsible, under the constitution, to
the Supreme Soviet, through its Presidium. Theoretically
the Presidium may break any minister at will. Theoretically the Presidium is responsible to the delegates of the
Supreme Soviet. Theoretically the Supreme Soviet is responsible to the electors. Thus, theoretically, the people
of Russia may sack any minister at will. But the chairman
of the Council of Ministers, or prime minister, is Stalin,
and immediately under him are the deputy chairmen, or
deputy prime ministers, the first of whom is Mr. Molotov.
Each of these vice-premiers supervises a group of minis-
tries, or a branch of state policy—as Beria, for example, is
responsible for all the police; Bulganin for the armed
forces; Mikoyan for trade. It is.they who, with Stalin, make
up the inner cabinet of the U.S.S.R.

But not, in practice, as deputy premiers. They owe their
place and power to quite another source than the Supreme
Soviet: the source to which the Supreme Soviet itself owes
its being. They owe it to the Communist Party; and not
even to the Communist Party as a whole, but to its innermost circle: in effect, to Stalin. And it is in their capacity
of members of the Political Bureau of the party's Central
Committee that they rule over all Russia and require
themselves to be appointed as constitutional ministers by
the Presidium of the Supreme Soviet, whose chairman is
one of their number. These are the notorious thirteen
men (actually the number varies from time to time, and
at the moment of writing there are twelve) who, with
Stalin at the head, are the absolute rulers of Russia.

The Central Committee of the Communist Party of the
U.S.S.R. now has seventy-one members, elected at the

party's periodical congress, or co-opted between congresses. There is supposed to be a congress every three years, but the last one was in 1939, so for twelve years the Central Committee has gone its own way in more or less total obscurity, filling its vacancies by its own choice—or, rather, by the choice of the general secretary, Stalin, or his nominees. Since seventy-one members are an unwieldy number for day-to-day business, the Central Committee elects various permanent subcommittees. These subcommittees are first the Politburo, which takes all policy decisions to do with the government of the U.S.S.R.; then the Orgburo, which is responsible for the organization of the party, with, at present, some six million members; then the Control Commission, which is responsible for the internal discipline of the party. Over and above these subcommittees there is a permanent Secretariat, which keeps a close eye on the work of them all. The first secretary, or secretary-general, is Stalin, who was appointed to this post by Lenin in 1922, and used it patiently, ingeniously, and ruthlessly to break his enemies and promote his friends. When, through the Secretariat, he had gained control over the whole Central Committee (which in those days was much smaller), it meant that he had control also of the Politburo, and therefore of Russia.

This, in very sketchy outline, is the pattern of the Stalin dictatorship. It is interesting enough for what it is; but far more interesting and relevant to our purpose is how it came to be what it is.

What we forget in our vision of unbridled despotism is that if the members of the Politburo are the lords of all Russia, they are also the creation of Russia, just as Hitler and his friends were also the creation of Germany, just as Messrs. Attlee and Truman are the proud creations of the Anglo-Saxon powers. Stalin and his colleagues did not spring armed with tommy guns from the head of Lucifer to batten on a stricken and defenceless land. They owe their very existence as tyrants to the people over whom they tyrannize. The Politburo in its present form was not a sudden inspiration but the product of an elaborate evolution. Lenin, who would regard it with horror and outrage, was nevertheless its begetter; and the nature of the Russian people, who groan beneath its scourge, enabled it to develop as it has developed. Just as we had to look to the Russian people to explain the triumph of Lenin, so we must look to them to show us Stalin.

2

The Inevitability of Stalin

THERE IS NO DOUBT at all that in 1917 Lenin believed
with all his soul that he was working towards an egalitarian
system under which there would be no exploiters and exploited and which would sooner or later do away with the
necessity for a bureaucratic state. Bureaucracy, in his view,
like the standing army, was no more than "a parasite created by the inherent antagonisms which rend society." Do
away with the antagonisms—the class antagonisms, of course
—and the parasite would die with them. This was called
the withering away of the state.

In 1917, just before the revolution, Lenin had no
thought at all of taking over the existing apparatus of the
state. The workers were to smash it and replace it with
their councils, or soviets; and although Lenin himself drew
the line at the assumption of some of his followers that the
whole administration of the country should immediately
be taken over by the mob, he was certainly convinced that
the word had only to be given for "the toilers, the poor,

to share in the day-to-day work of governing the state" in addition to earning their livings in the factories and the fields. In fact, his own early ideas of how to run a country are a commentary on his marked limitations as a practical man of affairs, limitations nowadays glossed over, even by his opponents (for these also are intent on creating a legendary figure of a benign and versatile genius to set against Stalin, his betrayer). In the organization of industry and finance, for example, he saw nothing beyond "the simple operations of registration, filing and checking which . . . can easily be performed by every literate person."

At the same time, as a natural autocrat, he was far too shrewd, when it came to the pinch, to allow that the higher direction of the revolution and the building of socialism should be entrusted to the masses, on behalf of whom the revolution had been made. He was not a Russian for nothing, and, by temperament domineering, he had inherited a tradition of centralism and rigid prescription from above. He, Lenin, was the higher direction of the revolution; and although he often asked the comrades what to do, if it was anything he felt strongly about (which, as a rule, it was), he very soon gave them the answer. In exile, to get his way, he had split the Social Democratic Party and risked reducing it to futility, quarrelling decisively with his oldest friends and preceptors, like Plekhanov. He got away with this by sheer force of personality. But when it came to running a country, a country, moreover, spread over half the world, force of personality was no longer enough. There had to be laws, and the means to enforce those laws. Both soon took on, inevitably, an extremely Russian flavour; and it is fascinating to see how even during the first flush of Bolshevik power the utopian dreams of the men who were going to do away with the whole paraphernalia of tsarist oppression, from prisons to colonies, from the church to the censorship, from privilege to marriage, were, from the very beginning, hamstrung by the fact that they could only find Russian answers to Russian problems, and counterbalanced by a strong authoritarian centralism curiously at odds with the free and unbridled discussion at all levels through which the management of the country was supposed to be effected.

"All Power to the Soviets!" had been the slogan of the October Revolution; and Lenin paid lip service to conventional democratic ideas by convening the long-promised Constituent Assembly. But it was convened only to be broken up forever. Lenin's ideas about parliamentary democracy had been exactly expressed in his pamphlet called *The State and Revolution:*

> To decide once every few years which member of a ruling class is to misrepresent the people in parliament is the real essence of bourgeois parliamentarianism, not only in parliamentary-constitutional monarchies, but also in the most democratic republics.

He was also quite clear in his mind that "All Power to the Soviets!" meant one thing to him and quite another to the masses who had spontaneously organized these soldiers' and workers' councils. To Lenin it meant power for the soviets to support the Bolshevik programme, not only in the teeth of reaction but also in the teeth of the other revolutionary parties; and the Bolshevik programme pivoted on an idea which made nonsense of the soviets. It took no stock in the political sense of the masses; and from the first days of the revolution there was manifest in Lenin's actions what must always appear to Western eyes that strange contradiction of cynicism and enthusiasm which is a feature of Russian politics. It is past all question that

Lenin was fanatically devoted to his cause, which was the liberation of the oppressed masses from their chains. At the same time, when it came to immediate practice, he regarded these same masses as no more than dupes or pawns in a skilled political manœuvre conducted by himself. He lied to them for their good. He lied so brazenly, telling them, for example, to seize the land, when he knew that soon he would be taking it back, telling them again that through their soviets they were governing the country, when he knew that he had them on a string—he lied so brazenly in what to him was supremely the good cause that the memory of it should make us reflect in face of some of Stalin's lies, which appear to us wanton and directed towards quite conscious evil.

The real power in the early stages of the revolution was to be the dictatorship of the proletariat. In Lenin's words:

> The "special repressive force" for the suppression of the proletariat by the bourgeoisie, for the suppression of millions of toilers by a handful of the rich, must be superseded by a "special repressive force" for the suppression of the bourgeoisie by the proletariat (the dictatorship of the proletariat).

But since the proletariat as a whole were politically unawakened, and nowhere more unawakened than in Russia (where they were also few, in a land which was then four-fifths peasantry), the effective dictatorship had to come from their politically advanced elements, "the vanguard of the proletariat." The politically advanced elements were, by definition, the members of Lenin's party, later to be known as the Communist Party, which thus came to exercise a dictatorship in the name of the proletariat and in trust for the masses. The idea was that sooner or later the vanguard would hand over responsibility to the main body. That idea was never fulfilled, and it never will be. While numerically the party has enormously expanded to take in a powerful cross section of the most gifted and active people in the land, qualitatively, by Lenin's standards, it has steadily declined; and with its numerical growth has gone an increasing concentration of power into the hands of the inner circle, the Central Committee and its subcommittees, which may thus be seen, in Lenin's jargon, to be the advanced guard of the vanguard, with the main body lost in the dust.

Even while Lenin was alive the ideas of ultimate equality began to fade. Having justified his own dictatorship—or, rather, dictatorship by committee, which it still was in his day—in quasi-Marxist terms, he stopped repining and threw himself with all his vigour into the new tyranny which had as its sole immediate object the retention of power. This was by no means an easy exercise. He not only had the civil war and the intervention on his hands, but also severe troubles with the very people to the service of whom his whole life had been dedicated. At first the Social Revolutionary Party, the non-Marxist revolutionary party of the countryside, was the chief opponent; and it was a Social Revolutionary, Dora Kaplan, who shot at Lenin in 1921, not killing him but directly causing his premature death in 1924. But soon the increase in power of the central dictatorship brought him into bitter conflict with faithful rank-and-file members of his own party. Nineteen-twenty-one was the critical year, and the conflict was symbolized by the rebellion in the naval dockyards at Kronstadt. Nobody had very much liked the closing down of the Constituent Assembly, in Trotsky's words, "a frank and complete liquidation of formal democracy in the name of the revolutionary dictatorship"; but at that time the people had other things to think about, such as the promised prospect of peace and the seizing of the land. When Lenin, announcing its dissolution, had exclaimed, "And now we have carried out the will of the people—the will that says all power to the soviets," the soviets, believing they had the power, had nothing much to say against it. But when the central government started requisitioning grain, it was quite another story (here again we see the people of Russia in revolt, not caring for political ideas, but only asking for bread and freedom to get on with their own lives); and the manifesto produced by the Kronstadt mutineers not only shows the sort of grievances that really mattered to them, but also, by implication, how far the dictatorship had travelled along the road to Stalin's Russia. Re-election of the soviets by secret ballot with free preliminary electioneering was the first point. Liberation of political prisoners of the Socialist Parties was another. Freedom of meetings, trade unions, and peasant associations. Freedom of speech for workers, peasants, anarchists, and Left Socialist Parties—though not by any means for everyone. And so on.

The Kronstadt rebellion was put down, as were many other less dangerous revolts; and gone were the days when leading Bolsheviks, like Zinoviev and Kamenev, had protested to the point of resignation at the development of police terror. Now a final drive was made against all the remaining Socialist opposition: "We shall either keep them safely in prison," wrote Lenin in May 1921, "or send them to Martov in Berlin for the free enjoyment of all the amenities of free democracy." By that year, the Cheka, the revival of the tsarist secret police, had been expanded to over thirty thousand; it had been started only six weeks after the revolution and originally consisted of Dzerzhinsky, later to be hymned as "the fearless knight of the revolution," and a few chosen assistants. And in that same year

Lenin himself proposed and secured the readoption of the death penalty for "membership or participation in an organization supporting that section of the international bourgeoisie that tries to overthrow the Communists."

Today when we compare the reality of Soviet Russia with Lenin's dream, it is all too easy to see what has gone wrong. What is not so easy to see, because the route traced by the march of progress is obscured by its own dust, is that the dream had been abandoned long before Stalin took over from Lenin.

In October 1917, on the eve of their *coup d'état,* the Bolsheviks had quite clear ideas about a number of things; and had Lenin been asked by an outsider what he proposed to do with his power when he got it, he would have given an eloquent and circumstantial answer. He was going to establish a republic of workers' and peasants' councils, or soviets, which, under his watchful eye, would form the real and effective government. If this system could be extended to the various minority nationalities which made up the tsarist empire, well and good; if not, no tears would be shed. The republic was to be a Socialist republic. In agriculture there would be cooperative farming on the larger estates; but the rest of the land would be given to the peasants to work as they saw fit, with the proviso that somehow they must be prevented from covering the countryside with a patchwork of uneconomical small holdings. In industry the workers would themselves take over control and devise their own managerial apparatus, in which free discussion would play an important part. Inequalities of pay would be drastically reduced, and the aim would be total equality: the Bolsheviks themselves would set an example in this direction, and the highest Bolshevik functionaries would receive no more than a manual worker. In the social sphere, women would be granted complete equality with men; and, although Lenin himself frowned on promiscuity, easy divorce and legalized abortion were to put an end to the subjection of the female by the male. In the arts, in education, in every sphere where the human mind may range, there would be untrammelled experiment. The whole apparatus of the state was to be smashed and never rebuilt; police, army, bureaucracy were all to be abolished. Prisons were to be abolished, because crime, like all other evils, was a product of the conflict of classes; since there would be no classes, crime would die out. In the initial stages of the revolution it might be necessary to segregate active opponents of the new régime, who might embarrass the building of the new society; but this necessity would pass if the revolution triumphed. Internationally, Russia as a power would cease to exist. Her place would be taken by the first Soviet Socialist Republic, and, fired by her example, the workers of Europe would rise everywhere in revolt and establish sister republics in their own lands.

This is a summary of Lenin's proclaimed intention. It was to fulfil this intention, and for no other purpose whatsoever, that he laboured a lifetime and put his convictions to the test by violence. So that when people talk nowadays about the success of the Russian Revolution, I do not know what they mean. Russia, as a power, has succeeded in surviving Lenin and becoming stronger than she was before. A group of men, headed by Stalin, have succeeded, personally, in the vulgar sense ("From bank robber to prime minister," as who should say, "From log cabin to White House"). It could be proved, I think, that some sort of revolution was necessary to transform Russia from an agrarian to an industrial state. But the revolution as Lenin saw it has totally and ignominiously failed.

Instead of a workers' and peasants' republic there is an

absolute dictatorship, made worse by the pretence (new to Russia, which is not given to self-deception) of democracy. Instead of independence for the nationalities there is absolute domination of them from the centre. Instead of socialism there is a system of state capitalism. Instead of a mixture of cooperative and free farming, there is the most rigid form of collectivization under which the peasant is being increasingly degraded, until, today, he is hardly more than a state serf. Instead of the workers controlling industry, they are subject to the harshest labour laws in the world drawn up by trade unions which have become an instrument of the central government, and driven by a new managerial class which regards its labour force in the same spirit as the early nineteenth-century millowners of Lancashire regarded theirs. Instead of equality of pay and the abolition of privilege, inequalities have become more marked than in any other country in the world outside the native states of India. The rule of privilege is absolute. Women have indeed achieved equality with men; but the chief function of this equality is to compel them to do the hardest and dirtiest manual labour. New marriage laws have put divorce increasingly out of reach; and the fecund mother, as in Hitler's Germany, is decorated as a heroine. The arts and education have become vehicles for Stalin's propaganda. The apparatus of state, police, army, and bureaucracy is the mightiest in history. Thirty years after Lenin, individuals classified as active enemies of the people are numbered in millions and segregated in labour camps, where they live and die in conditions of extreme misery. Russia as a power is the second strongest in the world, has subjugated many of her neighbours by force or the threat of force, and seeks actively and successfully to upset the balance of the world. No single country in Europe has been fired to revolt in sympathy; and where revolutions have occurred (never outside the Soviet field of influence), the most ardent Communists have afterwards been imprisoned or killed and replaced by Russian agents.

> Lenin and his followers set out to achieve for humanity the goals of freedom and equality by means of an organization which denied these same principles.

And again:

> While the ideology of ends has been much modified, or discarded, the ideology of means has had lasting importance.

In those two observations of Mr. Barrington Moore we have the beginning and the end of Lenin's revolution.

It was a quick end. The end of freedom came at the beginning. It could be argued that the dictatorship of the proletariat, as such, was not the end of freedom, since the workers and peasants were, as far as the Bolsheviks were concerned, the whole of the new society. But almost at once freedom vanished from within the new society, and workers and peasants whose last desire was to bring back the old order were subjected to strict discipline from above. We have seen in the Kronstadt rebellion how the disillusioned proletariat reacted against this development. But their resistance was in vain. Lenin had a formula for it: he could be relied upon to have a formula for everything he wanted to do, expressed in quasi-Marxist terms. When he glorified the power of theory, what he really meant was the power of jargon, of which, with the Viennese psychologists, he was the joint discoverer. The jargon phrase, by virtue of which he was able to turn on the proletariat and crush it, was "democratic centralism." "Abracadabra" would have meant just as much and been quicker to say, but "democratic" carried certain associations which were useful. "Freedom in discussion—unity in action" was Lenin's summary of this piece of high-powered nonsense. And on "Freedom in discussion—unity in action" the Soviet régime has been built. It meant in practice, once the Bolsheviks were in power, that it was a severe offence for anybody to criticize a line of policy which had been approved by the party congress. Therefore, by natural degrees, as the Central Committee centralized the party in itself, it became a severe offence for anybody to criticize a line of policy promulgated by the Central Committee. And this had the effect of diverting all discussion throughout the hierarchy of soviets—from the Supreme Soviet to the village soviet—from policy itself to the execution of policy, so that Socialist self-criticism, of which so much is made, has become an excellent way of finding scapegoats for the blunders of the Kremlin. If, for example, the Kremlin based a plan for grain production on the assumption that industry would turn out so many thousand tractors in excess of its capacity, the plan was never criticized, could *not* be criticized; but the wretched department responsible for tractor production could be freely criticized, in the press and in the soviets. Popular anger would thus be diverted from the Kremlin; a few heads would roll; and the plan would be quietly dropped. This is a technique not unknown to some of our own politicians; but outside the Soviet Union it has not yet been exalted into a system of government and given a fancy name.

"We have never rejected terror on principle, nor can we do so," said Lenin as early as 1901. Terror was indeed rejected by the Bolsheviks purely on grounds of expediency. They regarded the assassinations of the Social Revolutionaries with contempt: isolated acts of terror could achieve nothing and would in fact strengthen the hand of the enemy, besides diverting the minds of the revolutionaries from the serious work ahead. But once the Bolsheviks had power and could make use of terror on a large and effective scale, it at once became expedient to do so. The terror let loose on active opponents of the régime, and formally inaugurated in the autumn of 1918, very soon came in useful for the repression of those who opposed not the régime as such but also certain decisions of the government in detail—as provided for by the magic formula "democratic centralism." And the instrument forged to kill the counterrevolution was soon turned impartially against those proletarian heroes of the revolution who found themselves differing from the central government and dared to say so—as, for example, the Kronstadt mutineers.

Lenin himself was saved from his own logic by the diversion he created with his New Economic Policy of 1921, which he himself called "a partial return to capitalism." But although this gave the country as a whole a much-needed breathing space, within the party itself the dictatorial trend continued. At the Tenth Party Congress Lenin made it quite clear that he was not prepared to tolerate unlimited discussion, even under the head of "democratic centralism." In a passage which was to prove precious beyond rubies to his less outspoken successor, he attacked the practical application of what he himself theoretically allowed:

Probably there are not many among you who do not regard this discussion as having been an excessive luxury. Speaking for myself, I cannot but add that in my opinion this luxury was really absolutely impermissible; by permitting such a discussion we undoubtedly made a mistake and failed to see that in this discussion a question came to the forefront which, because of the objective conditions, should not have been in the forefront; we wallowed in luxury and failed to see the extent to which we were distracting attention from the urgent and menacing question of this very crisis that confronted us so closely.

At the same congress, a resolution was passed condemning factional groups within the party and empowering the Central Committee to root out and destroy such groups as soon as they showed their heads.

Anyone who has listened to a debate in the House of Commons, or Congress, at a time of crisis, will sympathize with Lenin. America and Britain have, so far, just got by because compromise is in the blood and a sense of proportion, in the last resort, comes to the rescue of the vast majority. But Russia, as we have seen, is impatient of moderation. Discussion means discussion to infinity. In Russia there is no qualifying mercy. The choice does not lie between too much discussion and too little discussion; it lies between discussion and no discussion. We cannot blame Lenin for behaving as he did; we can only blame him for thinking that he could behave in any other way, he being a Russian and knowing Russia. It is worth remembering that the Kronstadt mutineers, those symbols of Bolshevik oppression, while they themselves cried out to Lenin for free speech were careful to demand it only for themselves and their kind. . . .

It would be tedious, and it is quite unnecessary in a study of this kind, to trace in detail the development of the Kremlin dictatorship as we know it today. The point to be made is that it has developed remorselessly on lines clearly laid down by Lenin: Lenin in his struggle to govern the people of Russia, who can be governed only by naked force. It would be tedious because there is nothing to record but the endless repetition of a single elementary trick; and the whole monstrous history of the seizure and retention of power by the Bolsheviks, played out over the great Russian plain at the cost of bloodshed and famine and countless millions of ruined lives, all arrayed in the pedantic panoply of a discredited German theory of history, may be rendered by a single phrase of schoolboy English:

> The Bolsheviks used ideas; they did not serve them [to quote Mr. A. J. P. Taylor]. Take the question of "national freedom." The Bolshevik principle was very simple. National freedom was right when it operated to disintegrate bourgeois "imperialist" states; it was wrong when it threatened "the workers' state," that is, themselves. All Bolshevik morality, politics, and constitutions can be reduced to a single sentence: "Heads we win; tails you lose."

I have already quoted Stalin on one aspect of this very matter of national freedom. Here he is again:

> The proletariat should support nationalist movements which tend to weaken and subvert imperialism, not those which tend to strengthen and maintain it. In certain oppressed countries, nationalist movements may run counter to the general interests of the proletarian movement. Obviously there can be no question of our helping such movements as these. The problem of national rights does not stand alone; it is part of the general problem of the proletarian revolution, is subordinate to it, and can only be considered by the proletariat from that angle.

This is a longer essay in jargon than "democratic centralism"; but Stalin has always lacked Lenin's publicity agent's gift for misleading compression. "Heads I win; tails you lose" is shorter and more honest.

But it is Leninism, not Stalinism. It was Lenin who first applied the trick to the government of Russia. He tricked the workers and peasants into giving him their support by promising them peace and land—knowing that he was going to embroil them in "a series of bloody conflicts," knowing that sooner or later he would have to collectivize the land. It was Lenin who permitted the march on Warsaw "in order to defend the power of the working-class." It was Lenin who, with his New Economic Policy, first treated the world to the edifying spectacle of a revolutionary leader cooperating with those who most hated the revolution in order that he might more conveniently carry out the ruthless liquidation of all those revolutionary elements in the country who might spoil his own particular game.

In a word, the evolution of the Politburo into the most absolute and comprehensive dictatorship in modern history was inherent in Leninism, which supplied the technique; and it was made possible by the Russian people, who, during the years when it would still have been possible for a determined leader basing himself on a popular idea to break the Bolshevik tyranny, if only by mobilizing the people for passive resistance on a nation-wide scale, failed ignominiously to make themselves felt. There were potential leaders, at first in the open opposition, then in the underground opposition, later in the army and the Communist Party itself. But there was no popular idea for them to base themselves on; and this is the tragedy of Russia and the real cause of her backwardness. It is not a matter of machine guns. Alexander II had no machine guns. It is the lack of popular ideas. Popular ideas, popular beliefs in simple principles, may be silly and deluded;

but at least they take those in whose breasts they burn like a flame right out of themselves and turn them into the stuff of martyrs. Russia is the country without martyrs. There was plenty of passive and even active resistance in the first decade of Bolshevik rule. But it was not a resistance of principle: it was never a national movement to overthrow a tyranny which offended all the canons of decency. Russia is a country where decency plays no part: there is no accepted code of behaviour; no lowest common denominator of permissible conduct. All conduct is permissible; so that individual kindness, of which there is the greatest store in the world, is invariably opposed by organized evil. The early resistance to the Bolsheviks was foredoomed because it had no idea behind it, just as all the peasant revolts of Russian history had no idea behind them. Even the heroic Kronstadt mutineers, as we have seen, were not fighting for free speech in principle, but only for free speech in their own favour. The flame of martyrdom is not kindled by an overriding desire for bread and a quiet life. Sometimes, when bread is more than usually scarce and the pressure from the central government more than usually harsh, anger and desperation break out into revolt. But there is no momentum in such revolt, which must, in the end, acknowledge superior force and give in. So the character of the Russian people, which enabled Lenin to seize power, because they would not ardently support a provisional government which was trying, however ineffectually, to bring to Russia a genuinely democratic idea, also enabled Stalin to consolidate his grip.

As for the potential leaders of revolt, the men of his own party whom Stalin later shot—these were so imbued with the Russian belief in the saving power of orthodoxy that when they found they could not carry their opinions, they recanted, not to save their own skins but in order that the community might survive as a united body. So perhaps it is not fair to say that Russia is the country without martyrs. It is the country of a million martyrs. For the martyr, in Russia, is the man who destroys his own mind rather than allow it to flaw the perfect unanimity of the communal plan. At that rate it looks as though he is a man who sets the group above truth. And, indeed, he is precisely that. For what is truth? The search for truth can end only in the broadest approximations. For the Russian, the all-or-nothing absolutist, this is not enough. If he cannot attain to the absolute truth he has attained to nothing. This was the mood of the nineteenth-century exemplars of futility. Then, for a time, at the opposite pole, the Russian Bolshevik took Marxism for truth. But Marxism was no more than what the Marxists said it was, which meant, in practice, what the Kremlin Marxists said it was, men who were Russian by birth and Marxist by adoption. This, it is easy to see from our own position of detachment, meant nothing else than the rebirth of the Russian idea, for which, without knowing it, Bukharin died. But Stalin knew it, seeing more clearly, perhaps, because he himself was not a Russian.

3

The Perversion of an Idea

IF IT WAS LENIN who brought Russia into communism, it is Stalin who has taken Marxism out of Leninism. This is a statement which calls for a great deal of qualification; but since it is a key to our understanding of the motives of the Kremlin at this moment of time, I have put it at the head of this section as a signpost to the direction in which we are moving. I do not say that Stalin knew what he was doing when he began the process of extraction; but he certainly knows now. It is interesting to note that the very day on which that last sentence was written, my honoured acquaintance, Mr. Pospelov, lately editor in chief of *Pravda*, and now head of the Marx-Engels-Lenin Institute, made an oration, with Stalin on the platform, for the twenty-seventh anniversary of Lenin's death, in which the name of Marx was not mentioned once.

This does not prevent Stalin from making use of certain Marxist propositions, both inside and outside Russia (but especially outside); nor does it make him any the less an

97

unwitting prisoner of Marxist categories. He is certainly the last person in the world to underestimate the driving force of the Marxist-Leninist idea, an idea which dominates millions, who hardly realize their own subjection, and has been used to corrupt millions more. It is the sort of idea that has a magic appeal as a reach-me-down for any emergency, a sort of Children's Self-Instructor for Adults.

The power of the Marxist-Leninist theory lies in the fact that it enables the party to find the final orientation in any situation, to understand the inner connection of events, to foresee their course, and to perceive not only how and in what direction they are developing in the present, but also how and in what direction they are bound to develop in future.

That is a fair summary of what the doctrine means to believing Communists. It is taken from *A Short History of the Communist Party of the Soviet Union (Bolsheviks)*, at first said to be inspired by Stalin, who later claimed authorship. The language, taken at its face value, would suit an advertisement for a patent medicine. And the mentality it reveals is the mentality which seeks to explain all bodily ills in terms of night starvation. The fact that men believe in a philosophy does not make them philosophers; and we should be able to keep quite clearly in our minds the distinction between the men who use Marxism, or Marxist-Leninism, as a rule-of-thumb measure and the men who are capable of developing the theory. To believe in a theory which purports to explain the universe neither means that the theory really does explain the universe nor that the believer understands the theory, nor that he is capable of applying it in practice. For example, my own belief in Einstein's theory is just about as instructed as the average Communist's belief in Marxism—though rather

more tentative. In his brilliant biography of Stalin, Mr.
Isaac Deutscher gets very near the truth in a reference to
Stalin's Marxism which has all the dangerous contempt of
the intellectual for the man of action:

> Yet the interest of practitioners of Stalin's type in
> matters of philosophy and theory was strictly limited.
> They accepted certain basic formulas of Marxist philos-
> ophy, handed down to them by the popularizers of the
> doctrine, as a matter of intellectual and political con-
> venience. These formulas seemed to offer wonderful
> clues to the most complex problems—and nothing can
> be so reassuring to the half-educated as the possession of
> such clues. The semi-intelligentsia from whom social-
> ism recruited some of its middle cadres enjoyed Marx-
> ism as a mental labour-saving device, easy to handle,
> and fabulously effective. It was enough to press a knob
> here to make short work of one idea, and a knob there
> to dispose of another.

But although Mr. Deutscher gets very near the truth, it
seems to me that here, as everywhere, a miss is as good as a
mile. That passage applies with exactitude to the sort of
people whom Stalin has used, as, with the substitution of
two or three words, it would apply to the vast majority of
Christians; but it does not, I think, apply to Stalin himself. We do not know (and since we are not making a
psychological study of Stalin, it does not matter) whether
Stalin himself took the words of the passage cited above
at the value put upon them by others when they were written in 1928. I am inclined to think he did not: the passage
is riddled with carefully sited loopholes. What matters is
that he certainly does not today. This would be clear from
internal evidence alone; but since Stalin himself has lately

proclaimed it, we need no longer rely on internal evidence.

My own view, in the light of his revealed character, is that Stalin, unlike his senior colleagues, has always taken his Marxism with a grain of salt, as the mediæval popes (and, may we hope, some of the more recent ones too?) took their proclaimed dogmas. Although there is no documentation to show that Stalin did not swallow Leninist-Marxism whole until the year 1931, we have his actions to go on. And there has been nothing at all in Stalin's career to suggest either that he has the doctrinaire mentality or that he would, knowingly, swallow anything whole. Indeed, the available evidence all suggests the contrary. This does not mean, let me repeat, that his whole outlook is not coloured and, indeed, heavily conditioned, by Marxist modes of thought.

But before we grapple with the problem of what Stalin and his friends really believe, it is necessary to consider whether they believe anything at all. There is a school of thought which holds that they do not. And the interesting thing is that precisely those who regard the Politburo as a collection of unmitigated gangsters are those who talk most freely about the menace of communism. This confusion seems to arise from a sentimental fallacy. It is easy to think of these men as ingenious thugs, cruel, unscrupulous, unprincipled, intent on keeping their jobs, cost what it may, devoured by a craving for power, and nothing else besides. Without asking what a gangster really is, and whether in fact the gangster mentality is capable of a sustained interest in world dominion, let us accept the loose term. Certainly, then, the actions of the Politburo are cruel. Certainly these men have no scruples. Certainly their behaviour, by our standards, is unprincipled. Certainly they exhibit a deep and sustained concern for the

retention of their own positions. Certainly they find in the
exercise of power an irresistible attraction.

But what is all that supposed to prove? It could be
argued that their cruelty is the cruelty of callousness, not
of active malevolence. They inherit the Russian tradition
of unbridled and arbitrary violence, heightened by clumsiness and a deficient sense of proportion. Their lack of
scruple may be due to conscious wickedness; but it may
equally well be a tribute to logic. Unscrupulous behaviour
within the canon is a prerequisite of Marxist-Leninism,
itself the formation of a rigid and all-embracing principle.
Concern for one's job is a universal human failing and
may be encountered in its purest form among British cabinet ministers, American presidents, or provincial station-
masters all over the world. The craving for power is self-
evident: few men achieve power, and none keep it for
long, unless they desire it above all things. But to say that
a man craves for power tells me nothing about him at all,
except that in this one particular he is not like me. Thus,
on the existing evidence, to think of the gloomy denizens
of the Moscow Kremlin as a collection of international
gangsters dominated exclusively by considerations of personal gain is not only unjustified, but also the summit of
wishful thinking of the unhappiest kind—the gangster
being in so many ways more easy to deal with than the
fanatic. For a gangster is a law unto himself, operating
without any vestige of moral authority, and, as such, in
himself destructible. The orthodox Moscow Communist,
on the other hand, whatever he may mean by communism
and no matter how debased his personal character, founds
his whole case on moral authority; and the case cannot
be destroyed by striking at the man. The same is true of
the patriot. In a word, if the members of the Politburo believe in neither communism nor Russia, then they are

simply evil human beings operating in a moral vacuum; but if they do believe in communism or Russia, or both, then they are men, evil or not, possessed by an idea. And they may be relied on to behave as such.

This is most emphatically not an academic quibble: it bears closely on the definition of the enemy, and thus on our own fate. Yet in trying to forecast our fate we make do with the most woolly kind of thinking about the men who may determine it. A predisposing factor for calamity is unreasoning fear, the kind of fear which stimulates panic action. Too many of us fear the Kremlin in this way; but half our fear and almost all our paralysis, a paralysis punctuated by spasmodic jabs intended as self-defence, is due to the quite unwarrantable attribution to the Soviet leaders of contradictory and mutually exclusive characteristics. In one breath we denounce them as irresponsible tyrants concerned only for their own aggrandizement and liable at any moment to make a megalomaniac bid for world conquest by force of arms. In the next breath we denounce communism, with Moscow as its Rome, for its drive towards revolution all over the world. This sort of confusion engenders a state of superheated fright and supplies a Freudian answer to any attempt to see the Bolsheviks in normal human perspective. Such of their actions as cannot be explained easily in terms of communism are at once explained in terms of gangster acquisitiveness. This is trying to eat one's cake and have it: it cannot be done. Nobody, not even Molotov, can have it both ways all the time. If sometimes the members of the Politburo appear to do so, this is due partly to their own confusion and partly, on our part, to a confusion of motives and means: the tactics are gangster tactics; but the motives are not gangster motives.

We have to remember who these people were before

they reached their present deadly eminence (I am speaking now of the older generation of Bolsheviks, those who shared in the revolution and had to fight for their victory: the younger generation, which has grown up inside the tight governing circle of a great power, presents a special and endlessly fascinating study, which we cannot touch on here). They were genuine revolutionaries, who, for whatever dark and smoky reasons, were impatient with the existing order of things and were prepared to risk their lives in its overthrow. Certainly they never expected to find themselves exalted to the overlordship of all Russia. Although, to judge by their characters and records, their devotion to the Leninist cause was, like Lenin's own, inspired more by hatred of the oppressors than by love for the oppressed, they were sustained, as Bolsheviks, by a quasi-philosophical interpretation of history which, though preposterous as a system, contains much truth in detail and, moreover, has taken in finer intelligences than theirs.

It may be said that the ruthless struggle for power and the subsequent exercise of it have corrupted them utterly. But this seems to me to beg the question: what is corruptible will be corrupted, and it may be taken as axiomatic that the seeker after power is a taker rather than a giver (nor matter how high-flown his ultimate aims), and, as such, was born corruptible. Certainly each and every member of the Politburo has been corrupted as a human being; but this is no reason to suppose that his habits of thought have been changed, which is all that need concern us here. The worldly prelate dies with a prayer on his lips, and means it; but he has not lived his belief. Even those among the Bolsheviks who have moved farthest from Marxism in their actions may still think unconsciously in Marxist terms. Indeed, it is impossible for them to think in any other terms, since they know no others. The gift of intellectual detachment is the rarest gift under the sun. Men cannot go on saying the same thing for decade after decade without becoming enmeshed by the words they have spun. Actually there is no evidence at all that Stalin's colleagues have ever tried to detach themselves. All the evidence goes to show that they are not only convinced exponents of what they take to be Leninism, but also its creatures.

As they understand it, it has brought them a great deal. It brought about the October Revolution; raised the Bolsheviks to absolute power over one-sixth of all the land in the world; enabled them to strike down their enemies and consolidate their régime; extended Moscow's effective dominion far beyond the borders of the Soviet Union; and heavily embarrassed the efforts of the Western powers (the enemy, by Soviet definition) to save what is left of Europe from the ruin of war. In Asia they are triumphing and making increasingly untenable the Far Eastern interests of England, France, and Holland. . . . How can they possibly fail to believe in the formula which has brought them all this? The fact that it has completely failed to achieve the one thing it was originally intended to achieve —namely, a decent life for the people of Russia—counts for nothing in the balance. There is always tomorrow. The fact that when they speak of communism, Stalin and his friends now mean Russia, or, more specifically, Great Russia, does not in the least prevent them from believing, somehow, that Marx is on their side.

The practice of holding two diametrically opposed ideas is so universal that it should call for no comment. We see it in our friends, and we see it in ourselves. Indeed, it is so much the mark of the human being that it may be seen as the infallible sign distinguishing man from the animal, which can only think one thing at a time. And yet it is

invariably disregarded. In this case, *either* the rulers of
Russia must be Marxists, or quasi-Marxists, *or* they must
be old-fashioned Great Russian imperialists, *or* they must
be gangsters. The truth, of course, is that they are all three
together. To take a concrete example: when Mr. Molotov,
with the bleakly triumphant air of a Socialist sanitary in-
spector condemning the servants' quarters of a palace, de-
clares, as he did in 1948, that "all roads lead to communism," what he really means is that all roads lead to Moscow; but the argument on which he bases this prognostica-
tion is a Marxist-Leninist argument. He knows no other.
And, even more importantly, the statement is based not on
observed fact but on a train of reasoning starting from a
premise which Moscow itself has proved false.

It is easy enough, looking round the world, to know
what Molotov thinks. What is not so easy to grasp is that
he is not a free agent in his thinking. There are moments,
these days, when to all of us those words seem only too
true. But the important thing about Molotov is that his
conviction is not derived from events, which show communism to be very much on the march, but from a theory
of history which insists that all roads *must* lead to communism. Thus, what is going on in the world today, from
the nationalist movements in Asia to the Marshall Plan
(seen as a desperate attempt by American big business to
prop up a tottering economy by forcing foreigners to con-
sume its products) only confirms what Molotov previously
knew. And the fact that the theory upon which his train of
reasoning is based has been completely shattered by
Lenin's revolution, which was not the sort of thing Marx
had in mind at all, and by what has happened in Russia
since, does not in the least diminish its validity in the eyes
of the man who knows no other way of reasoning.

As far as the world outside Russia is concerned, Stalin's

Marxism, Marxism already adapted by Lenin, as we have seen, contains only two principles which need affect us: the general proposition of the advancing proletarian revolution and the particular proposition which lays down the manner of its advance. This, indeed, is all that is left of the Kremlin's Marxism: all the rest, as we shall see, has gone aground on the hard reality of Russia and been finally abandoned. Even these two propositions have gone aground, and one day the Communists will be forced to recognize the fact—as, at least up to a point, Stalin himself already does. But by the bulk of the Moscow Communists they are not abandoned. We cling to our mistakes when we have nothing else to cling to; and a man who for years has looked at the world through the distorting glass of a dogma will tend to find confirmation of that dogma in everything he sees. He is denied objective vision. Thus, if since the last war the Communists in the international sphere (but not in Russia) may seem to have done very well, this is mainly because what is going on in the world today may be seen, in part, as conforming fairly closely to what could be happening according to Lenin, who remarked, for example, that Paris would fall on the Yangtse. Thus the appropriate dogmatic actions of the Kremlin may appear to produce the foreseen effects and may even, in some particulars (so close at certain points is the correspondence between theory and reality) actually do so. For example, if you believe that your neighbour has designs on a corner of your land and, taking preventive action to keep him at arms' length, provoke a retaliatory raid, then you will almost certainly take it as proved that your original fear was justified. And this is the sort of situation which the Moscow Communist is never tired of multiplying. It springs from a habit of mind, the origins of which we have examined. But this habit of mind does

not in the least preclude the development of views which
are logically incompatible with it, in this case the rebirth
of straightforward nationalism. Considering the illogical-
ity of our own individual behaviour, it is odd that we continue to demand logic in others, even to the point of distorting their actions to endow them with a logic which
does not exist. It can also be dangerous.

4

Russian Nationalism Reborn

Looking back in the light of recent events, it is possible to trace the rebirth of the Russian idea to the year 1931, when, in an impassioned speech to the men responsible for carrying out the first Five-Year Plan, Stalin threw aside his Marxist arguments and appealed directly to the national spirit. Certainly at that time something had to be reborn. As far as the people of Russia were concerned, the idea of the proletarian revolution leading to an age of liberty and light for the common man had broken down. Stalin had achieved absolute power as the result of a struggle which had all the characteristics of the old-fashioned palace intrigue, in which one man's wits are set against another's and the impersonal forces of history appear to play no part at all. He had used Kamenev and Zinoviev to overthrow Trotsky; he had then used Rykov and Bukharin to overthrow Kamenev and Zinoviev; he was now strong enough to act in his own right and drop Rykov and Bukharin. His able and trusted right hand, Molotov, was to be made prime minister before the year was out, emerging from the obscurity of the Central Committee to be head of the constitutional government, and seizing the first occasion to proclaim his true functions to the listening world:

> I do not cease [he was to say] to be a party worker; and from now on I regard it as my primary function to carry out the will of the Central Committee.

That meant the will of Stalin, as secretary-general. For Stalin, in his fight for power, had contrived to pack the higher reaches of the party with his own supporters, who owed everything to him. This was not a Marxist conception of the nature of government in a Socialist society. Nor was it a Leninist conception, although its fulfilment had been made possible by nobody but Lenin.

At the same time, Stalin had just forced Russia through the collectivization of agriculture at the cost of a civil war between the government and the peasants. Lenin had seen the necessity for what he called cooperative farming; but at the time of the N.E.P. he thought it would take twenty years to reach the stage when the peasantry could be placed "squarely on a Socialist footing." Stalin decided to rush through the full-scale collectivization once and for all, basing his decision on the need to bring agriculture to the point where it could, with reduced manpower (for the men were needed in the factories), ensure sufficient and more reliable supplies for the town workers. He did force it through, but at a fearful price, which the Russians are still paying. First there were the millions of ruined lives, the lives of the rich and middle peasants, the so-called kulaks, killed in the struggle or exiled to Siberia; then the three million dead in the great famine which swept the Ukraine, when the peasants burnt their crops and slaughtered their livestock rather than deliver them to the government—a calamity which halved the farm animals throughout the Soviet Union and which had still not been made good when the Germans attacked ten years later; finally the permanent embittering of the peasants, especially in the west, which had all but fatal results in the first two years of the war.

At the same time the first Five-Year Plan was breaking down. Lenin had seen in the industrialization of the Soviet Union the only hope for the survival of the revolution. He had been forced to postpone it because of the deplorable state of industry after the civil war and the intervention, seeking the help of the N.E.P. men to get the country on its feet. By 1927 gross industrial production had been brought up to the prewar level, though there were bad patches, while grain production still lagged. Some sort of organized effort was now necessary, and in 1928 Stalin abolished the N.E.P. and launched the first Five-Year Plan, which was crazily overambitious. The plan and the collectivization went together. Both these policies, enforced industrialization using directed labour, and enforced collectivization, had been urged by Trotsky, and Stalin had already used the natural resistance to Trotsky's violence, notably as expressed by Bukharin, to rouse opinion against his major rival. But with Trotsky gone he proceeded to steal his thunder, destroying with his brutal and sustained attack on the old peasant economy, and by his slave-driving of the peasants forced into the new factories, the last vestiges of any pretence that the government was on the side of the people.

As if all this was not enough, the proletarian revolution had failed throughout Europe. Instead of Leninism there was fascism and nazism. And, with Russia in the throes of the most violent industrial and agrarian revolution in history—a revolution carried out from above in the teeth of popular resistance—Stalin found himself faced in the West with the new menace of Hitler, and in the East with the revived menace of Japanese imperialism.

Thus, by 1931, Stalin had proved in his own person that history was made not only by the impersonal interplay of social forces but also by the highly personal ambitions of individual leaders. He had also demonstrated to the people of Russia, finally and irrevocably with the liquidation of peasant resistance to collectivization and the introduction of penal labour laws, that they had no voice in the ultimate government of the country, and thus that the revolution, from this point of view, had been in vain. It had also been proved by the Germans and the Italians that the national idea had a far stronger appeal than the idea of international brotherhood. And so he now found himself in the absurd position of an absolute dictator basing his appeal on a palpable fiction which denied the possibility of his own existence and had no popular appeal, confronted with twin threats from the East and the West by absolute dictators whose positions were firmly based on genuine popular emotions.

Something had to be done. The first thing to be done was to get the Russian people to believe in him and to revive their ancient patriotism. This was not easy when they were all taught at school that great men did not exist and national pride belonged to the primitive past. Lenin would sooner or later have been faced with the same problem; but Lenin was spared by the merciful hand of death. Stalin, however, did very much exist; and he proposed to continue existing for a long time to come. As far as the unlettered masses were concerned, there was nothing to worry about. He, a Georgian by birth, and a politician of genius, knew all about the Russians, their profound love

of their native soil and their devouring need to believe in
a Little Father, a leader, quasi-divine, who would protect
them from the worst excesses of the officials. But the party
was another matter. The party with its radical Marxist
training, and on which he utterly depended when it came
to running the country, expected him to behave in a certain way. He could do pretty well everything with the
party that could be done by skilled manipulation; but he
could not without a serious upset stand up in front of it
and offer himself as the God-given leader of the Russian
people. For them he had to be the general secretary, wiser
than other men (because even Leninism expected some
men to be wiser than others: Lenin had set *that* precedent), more experienced than other men, but still the servant of the party. It would take some years before he could
appear in public as the Leader. In fact, from 1931, it took
exactly a decade plus the impact of a war. But at least he
could prepare the ground. And the best way to prepare the
ground was to revive the idea of Russia's destiny and the
idea of the great man.

I am not in the least suggesting that Stalin consciously
and lucidly held these thoughts. Indeed, he seems to be
above all a creature of instinct. But this, in fact, is what his
actions amounted to. If one saw Stalin as the cold-blooded,
timeless calculator, it would be possible to argue that his
plan of campaign went back to the day of Lenin's funeral,
when he inaugurated the Lenin cult, thus establishing a
precedent for great men.

But all the evidence suggests that he has lived very
much from hand to mouth, relying on instinct to tell him
broadly what to do and on an unbrookable will to com-
pensate for the blunders of execution. His sudden and improvised approaches to all the great crises of his life bear
out this reading, which indicates that he owes his present

stature to Russia far more than Russia owes her present shape to him. In so far as he broke away from the strait jacket of Marxist theory, it would be truer to say, I think, that the prime cause was (as he saw it) in the shortcomings of his fellow Marxists rather than in the shortcomings of Marxism as such. That is to say, standing a little apart and looking at his somewhat ridiculous colleagues with those appallingly shrewd Caucasian eyes, he saw that they were talking nonsense and were not at all the sort of men to put a great country on its feet and run it, least of all Russia. He alone had the strength, the character, the stamina, the flexibility required for such a task; and for him, whether consciously or not, theory was far more useful as a means of rationalizing the accomplished fact than as a guide to future action. He was not, most decidedly not, a Russian; he came of Georgian mountain stock which regarded its Russian conquerors with contempt as ponderous hobbledehoys. As for the Russian Jews, with their doctrinaire word-spinning . . . He was also, as we have seen, a man of the underground, who had stayed to fight again; and he had the distrust of the underground for the high-flown exiles.

Obviously this man had always been boundlessly ambitious. Just as obviously he did not seek deliberately to impose himself on Russia as its autocrat. There is good reason to believe that he suffered under the bitter condemnation of the dying Lenin, who saw too late where his junior colleague was heading—where he must inevitably head as the outcome of what he, Lenin, had done. Lenin, indeed, probably saw more clearly then, in those last months of his life, lying helpless, than Stalin himself could see. He did not set out to rule the people with an iron hand. We find him with his lieutenant, Kaganovich, racking his brain with an almost touching naïveté over the problems of democratic centralism. "If a deputy of a soviet goes to a meeting and knows beforehand that all questions and decisions have been already decided by a narrow committee of the party, he won't show much liveliness," Kaganovich had remarked in 1925. But by 1930 he had come to this: "One might say that this is a violation of proletarian democracy" (with reference to Stalin's own packing of the All-Union Council of Trade Unions), "but, comrades, it has long been known that for us Bolshevik democracy is not a fetish; for us, proletarian democracy is a means for arming the working-class for the better execution of its Socialist tasks."

The journey between those two attitudes was Stalin's own unpremeditated journey. From the sudden seizing of the initiative at Lenin's death, which largely depended on keeping Trotsky away from the funeral; through the unprepared attack on industry and agriculture, born of the realization that if something radical was not done immediately the Soviet Union would simply break up; through the clean sweep of the purges, which followed a genuine reluctance to kill or even imprison his opponents; through the pact with Hitler when all attempts at staving off war seemed to have failed; right down to the postwar decisions to exploit, cost what it might, the European chaos—from the beginning to the end there is nothing but improvisation on one elementary theme, stated vaguely at first, but with increasing clarity and resonance: the survival, then the glorification, of the Soviet Union.

The implications of that theme were made dramatically clear to all the world in August 1939, when, in an atmosphere of high spirits then unprecedented in the Kremlin, Molotov signed his pact with von Ribbentrop. But the theme itself was not formally stated until the war had been won and the Soviet Union had become a dominant power.

Then arose the cry that the first loyalty of all Communists everywhere was to the Soviet Union; and Stalinism had reached its apogee.

The programme of the Communist Party of the Soviet Union, the object of our struggle and the principles of Soviet foreign policy coincide with the general direction of the development of mankind. . . .

The best interests of all progressive forces throughout the world are identical with the interests of Soviet policy. . . .

In our epoch, in which all roads lead to communism, all those who declare themselves for the Soviet Union are historically correct. All those who declare themselves against the Soviet Union are historically incorrect. They are trying to arrest the wheels of history. This cannot be done, and all who attempt it will be broken and crushed by the march of history. . . .

Every victory of our Soviet Fatherland is a victory for progress and peace.

That is the most recent authoritative summing up of the ideological basis of the claim. It occurs in the official Soviet historical journal, *Problems of History,* for January 1950.

It may be answered that there is nothing new in this: Lenin expected all Communists everywhere to look to the Moscow Central Committee for instructions. So he did; but Lenin was still thinking in terms of the Communist International, with its headquarters in Moscow, not of the Soviet Fatherland. In those days Communists all over the world were required to obey the instructions of Moscow in order that their own local revolutions might be hastened. Today Communists all over the world are required to place themselves at the service of the Soviet state, a great power among great powers. There is a difference, as the Kremlin's treatment of Marshal Tito clearly indicates. It is a difference overlooked by contemporary Communists and even by opponents of communism, who see it as the most natural thing in the world that Communists should look to Moscow, as all Christians once looked to Rome. They ignore two facts: first, that loyalty to Rome was based on a divine sanction, as generally understood; second, that Rome did not set herself up as the capital of a secular power seeking ascendancy over other secular powers.

The use of the term "Soviet Fatherland" in the passage I have just quoted is calculated and deliberate. And the progress from the early days of the Comintern to the glorification of Great Russia, thinly disguised as the Soviet Union, and no longer disguised at all as the Communist Party, is easy to trace. It began, as I have said, with Stalin's speech to the industrial leaders in February 1931, in which he threw aside the conventional invocation of the revolution and made his passionate bid for a supreme effort with an appeal to Russian patriotism:

> No, comrades . . . the pace must not be slackened! On the contrary, we must speed it up to the limit of our powers and possibilities. This is dictated to us by our obligations to the workers and the peasants of the U.S.S.R. It is dictated to us by our obligations to the working class of the whole world.
>
> To slacken the pace would mean to lag behind; and those who lag behind are beaten. We do not want to be beaten. No, we do not!

The history of Russia, he went on to say, was the history of Russian defeats due to Russian backwardness:

She was beaten by the Mongol Khans. She was beaten by the Turkish Beys. She was beaten by the Swedish feudal lords. She was beaten by the Polish-Lithuanian *Pans*. She was beaten by the Anglo-French capitalists. She was beaten by the Japanese barons. *All* beat her because of her backwardness—military backwardness; cultural backwardness; political backwardness; industrial backwardness; agricultural backwardness. She was beaten because to beat her was profitable and could be done with impunity.

You remember [he continued] the words of the pre-revolutionary poet: "Thou art poor and thou art abounding. Thou art mighty, and thou art helpless, Mother Russia."

We are fifty or a hundred years behind the advanced countries. We must make good this lag in ten years. Either we do it or they crush us.

As events turned out, Stalin had precisely ten years and five months before the test was to come.

It is clear enough that by the time he made this speech and opened the way for the rewriting of Russian history, Stalin must have been developing his final conception of himself as the God-given leader. And I think we must agree with Mr. Deutscher that "he saw himself not as a modern Pharaoh but as a new Moses leading a chosen nation in the desert." Mr. Deutscher goes on to quote, by way of analogy, Macaulay on Cromwell and the Round-heads:

That singular body of men was, for the most part, composed of zealous republicans. In the act of enslaving their country, they had deceived themselves into the belief that they were emancipating her. The book which they most venerated furnished them with a precedent which was frequently in their mouths.

It was true that the ignorant and ungrateful nation murmured against its deliverers. Even so had another chosen nation murmured against the leader who brought it, by painful and dreary paths, from the house of bondage to the land flowing with milk and honey. Yet had that leader rescued his brethren in spite of themselves; nor had he shrunk from making terrible examples of those who contemned the proffered freedom, and pined for the flesh-pots, the task-masters and the idolatries of Egypt.

The patriotic idea to which Stalin was now appealing was at odds with the whole teaching of Marxist-Leninism. The foremost Soviet historian at that time was Pokrovsky, who had rewritten the history of Russia in Marxist terms. For him the history of the tsars was an indistinguishable part of general history, with no special significance, and of interest solely in so far as it could be made to reveal the working of Marx's "iron law." With the revolution, the people of Russia had been reborn, and the more darkly the past could be painted the more brightly the future would shine. Stalin's idea of the tsars as valiantly defending a backward people against the foreign invader was something totally new to people who had been taught for fourteen years that the tsars had been vile oppressors battening on their helpless subjects in league with the rulers of all the world. Further, in Pokrovsky's hands all the burning issues which for generations had divided the Russians and which must still divide them, since they arose from their deepest instincts—above all the pull, which I have already discussed, between Holy Russia and the dazzling West—counted for nothing at all. The past, as a formative influence, was a complete blank. To quote from Dr. Klaus Mehnert:

> Thus, pre-revolutionary Russia, as painted by the Pokrovsky school, was like a prison in which the people languished under the cruel and brutal depotism of the tsars. For them, the old disputes which for two centuries had split the Russian intelligentsia—the question whether the Russians belonged to the West or were a people apart—simply did not exist. Pokrovsky rejected the capitalist West and the imperialist fantasies of the Slavophiles impartially. For him the dawn of humanity began with the Bolshevik revolution. And this was the official line of the Soviet Union until 1934.

Dr. Mehnert, in his remarkable essay, *Weltrevolution durch Weltgeschichte,* traces with care and meticulous documentation the whole development which we are now discussing; but since he is working exclusively from the angle of Russian historical studies, he dates the rebirth of the Russian idea from the proscription of Pokrovsky in 1934. We have seen how Stalin, in 1931, made that event inevitable in a political speech about the Five-Year Plan to an audience of industrialists, which made nonsense of all Marxist historical teaching. But it is worth observing that the teaching went on undisturbed for another three years. Stalin had sown the seed of the new idea; but for three years it lay apparently unheeded. Then, suddenly, things began to happen. This is not the only instance of a contradiction between Stalin's utterances and general Soviet usage remaining unresolved for a long period. We should remember that sometimes today.

In the very year 1931 in which Stalin sowed his seed, another historian, Eugene Tarlé, was most violently denounced as "a bourgeois Russian historian, an imperialist, a chauvinist of the first world war, an ideological lackey of the imperialist front against the Soviet Union." This was because he showed signs of holding to an interpretation of Russian history not unlike that for which Stalin was preparing the ground. In the following year Pokrovsky died. He was given a state funeral and buried with all honour in the pantheon of Soviet heroes, the Kremlin wall behind Lenin's mausoleum. Then nothing happened for two years, when, without apparent warning, the Kremlin issued a decree pronouncing anathema on the late hero, banning his works, and describing him as "an enemy of the people, a despicable Trotskyite agent of fascism." Into the breach moved Eugene Tarlé, to all appearances lucky to be alive after his public disgrace of three years earlier. And the transformation of Russian history under the ægis of the late ideological lackey of the imperialist front against the Soviet Union began at once. Professor Tarlé, in his ripe old age, is still charmingly with us today, as a feature of every peace congress, used by Stalin, as the late Sergei Vavilov was used by him in the scientific sphere, to propagate ideas which have moved a very long way from the change of line that gave him his great chance.

One other thing happened in 1931: the return, as Dr. Mehnert points out, of two words, long banished from the language. The first was *rodina,* which is best translated as fatherland, but which has no exact English equivalent, with its conveyed image of the life-bearing earth, and which has no conceptual relationship with the word *otyechestvo,* often used in the phrase "the fatherland of socialism." The second was *patriotism.* Both occurred in a *Pravda* leading article glorifying the Soviet citizen as a fighter "for the fatherland, for its honour, glory, power and well-being." And, *Pravda* added, "Defence of the fatherland (*rodina*) is the highest law of life."

Meanwhile the new historians were set to work rewriting history in an essentially anti-Marxist sense, though still in Marxist terms. It was to take five years before the Pokrovsky interpretation was officially demolished in detail; and meanwhile, the idea of fatherland and patriotism having been firmly planted, the first task of the historians was to develop the idea of the great man. Stalin required a precedent and a lineage. The great men chosen as symbolic figures were, above all, Ivan the Terrible and Peter the Great; and their lives were to be rewritten so that both might be presented as direct forerunners of Stalin: Russian statesmen of infinitely farsighted vision who had taken upon their shoulders the burden of welding the unorganized might of the Russian people into a coherent and tempered force to withstand the assaults of a jealous and treacherous world. Their greatest enemy was treason; and they had not shrunk from the sternest measures to root it out, measures which had earned them in the eyes of an uncomprehending world an undeserved reputation for tyranny and cruelty. Only now, from the lofty eminence to which they had been brought by Stalin, were the Russian people able to look back and, from their new unity, appreciate the tremendous part played by these great men in laying the foundations of a great and proud nation. One of the most important essays in this field has been Professor Wipper's life of Ivan the Terrible. Wipper had started writing about Ivan in 1922 in the then-accepted manner. In 1942 he produced a revised version, prefaced by a modest little note which gives the unwary reader no indication at all of the magnitude of the revolution in his own approach: "The first edition of my essay *Ivan Grozny* was published in 1922. The subsequent appearance of new sources and of original works by U.S.S.R. historians prompted me to revise my work and to publish it in a new and enlarged edition." The general drift of the new interpretation can best be indicated by Wipper's own attack on the nineteenth-century historians, which is also an attack on his own past opinions:

> All these suffer from a defect which played a fatal rôle in establishing Grozny's reputation. They were perfectly indifferent to the growth of the Moscow State, its great unifying mission, Ivan IV's broad designs, his military innovations and his brilliant diplomacy. To some extent these judges of Ivan Grozny resemble Seneca, Tacitus and Juvenal who, in their sharp attacks on the Roman despots, concentrated their attention on court and metropolitan affairs and remained indifferent to the vastness, the borderlands, the external security and the glory of the celebrated empire.

Those words, which might occur in a well-conceived apologia for Stalin, appeared, as I have said, in 1942. It took the war to bring them out, just as it took the war to bring Stalin out as the supreme leader of his country, of the Soviet Fatherland. But the ground had been well prepared.

Thus, when, also in 1942, the army went back to golden epaulettes, the Guards were re-created, and new orders were named after warrior saints and tsarist generals, this was not the outcome of a sudden opportunist move. It had been well pondered. The outside world, as well as the Russian people, were quite right in believing that Stalin had moved away from Marxism and was reviving the old imperial idea with himself as the great *Vozhd* in place of the tsar. Our error was to attribute this process to the strains and stresses of war. It would, I believe, be more correct to say that the war gave Stalin a pretext for an open and wholehearted return to the Russian idea than to say that the war forced it upon him: it had already been forced upon him by the whole monstrous weight of Russia. But he was in the position of an atheistical Archbishop of Canterbury, the prisoner of his clergy. The sheep dogs were trained to certain methods and ends: they knew nothing else. The methods and ends in the shepherd's mind were changing; but he had no other dogs. In the stress of war, once the behaviour of the Germans had made it impossible for the Russian people to do anything but fight back (and it was more than a year before this happened as a general rule), in the uncomplicated act of resistance to a foreign invader Stalin was able to do without a great deal of the elaborate apparatus of coercion provided by the party and to rally the people round him as the supreme warrior chief. But when the war came to an end and the old peacetime treadmill had to be resumed, his figure was no longer enough in itself, and the whole apparatus of party and police had to be purged, restored, and strengthened.

There followed a passage which, more than anything else, lies behind our present misunderstanding of Stalin's true frame of mind: a vociferous return to Leninist teaching. The martial banners were put away; the victorious generals were removed from the public view; most interesting of all, the *Historical Journal,* which had been in the forefront of the nationalist movement since the banning of Pokrovsky, was wound up and replaced by a new review called *Problems of History,* which, in its first number (January 1945), formally attacked the "trend towards great power chauvinism" now discovered in its predecessor and promised to reverse the process which had been bringing back "bourgeois conceptions into the presentation of the growth of the Russian state," which had been "denying the revolutionary significance of the peasant movements, idealizing men of the autocratic order, and giving up the class analysis of historical phenomena." In 1946 Stalin made his celebrated speech, his only speech since the victory speeches of 1945, putting the war into Leninist perspective, warning his audience that the defeat of Germany did not mean the end of all war, invoking the Marxist interpretation of the nature of war, and laying down the outlines of a further industrial effort, to take "three more Five-Year Plans, I should think, if not more. . . . Only under such conditions can we consider that our homeland will be guaranteed against all possible accidents."

This speech, together with much that has followed— above all the foundation of the Cominform—came at the worst possible time for our understanding of Russia. I say this because it is only during the past four years that politicians and officials have taken to reading the Soviet scriptures; and Stalin's apparent return to the first principles of Leninism coincided with the popularization of Stalin's own early writing on the first principles of Leninism, including the long-term strategy of the world revolution. Stalin's apparent return to these principles was precisely what a reading of these works, without an understanding of Russian conditions, would lead one to expect. And this has been taken as final proof of the existence of a master plan running beneath all the deviations of the past thirty years. From this it follows that everything Stalin has done since 1924, and will in future do, is part of this plan. And the upshot is that we have frightened ourselves into hysteria with a chimera of our own imagination. In the next section I shall try to show that in the light of recent Soviet actions the idea of a master plan simply will not hold water. But for the moment we are still considering ideas.

There were, as I see it, three separate and strong reasons for the public revival of Leninist teaching after the war. The party, the best part of it, still believed in Marxist-Leninism; and so did the Soviet fifth column in the Communist Parties all over the world. To secure a firm grip on the countries belonging to his new sphere of influence in Eastern Europe, Stalin had to use the local Communists. These were not interested in the glory of Russia; they were interested in the advance of the Leninist revolution in their own countries. If their services were to be turned to Stalin's account, they had to be addressed in the language they best understood. This was the language of Leninism. Further, although, as I shall later try to show, the conception of the Cold War did not mature until 1947, and then only under the pressure of events, there is no doubt at all that Stalin saw in the Communist Parties of the West assets of great value in the general struggle for the glory and security of the Soviet Union. Messrs. Togliatti and Thorez were not kept in training by Moscow for nothing. At the same time it is important to remember that agents trained in Moscow may be intended by their master to serve ends very different from the ends they themselves imagine they are serving.

Stalin is still enough of a Marxist, and will always remain so, to be obsessed with the disintegrating tendencies of the modern capitalist society, and with the conviction that its instability, expressed in booms and slumps and the desperate struggle for markets, must sooner or later lead to wars of survival in a competitive world. This is certainly the Marxist teaching; but one does not have to be a Marxist-Leninist to see, for example, that at least a strong contributory factor in the rise of Hitler was the American policy which called for unlimited exports and restricted imports—a policy bound up with the problem of overproduction. Anybody who has been trained as a

Marxist will inevitably find the "internal contradictions" in the capitalist world obscuring his consciousness of all the other aspects of that world. It is in this sense, and in this sense only, that Stalin may still be called a Marxist.

The second reason for the open return to Leninism was, as I have already suggested, because Stalin needed at home a disciplined organization with a tempered cutting edge and a faith more compact and dynamic than a simple love of country. He needed this as an essential instrument in pushing Russia through the arduous years of sacrifice that lay ahead before she could feel safe from all outside interference. The only organization available was the Communist Party, and there was only one way of making it more efficient and self-conscious: by invoking the Leninist tradition. In other words, the purge of the party and the brushing up of its original ideology was, in effect, an evangelizing, or revivalist, movement conducted for political reasons by a man who was himself no believer. Lenin, as we have seen, had set plenty of precedents for this sort of behaviour; so, through history, had the religious and secular powers of every country in the world. It was not for nothing that Stalin had learnt from Marx that religion may be an instrument of government. But, instead of opium, Stalin gave his people Benzedrine.

The third reason was that Stalin had to consider the future. At the end of the war he was only sixty-five, but he had led a life of almost intolerable strain and the war had aged him and tired him. Towards the end of 1946 he fell dangerously ill, although this was concealed. He might, with his constitution of a Caucasian brigand, live for another thirty years; but, equally well, he might die at any time. He was a patriot for Russia: on the very lowest level of human experience, no man who had worked and fought as he had worked and fought to turn the Soviet Union into a great power, even if his underlying motive had been personal ambition, would willingly contemplate its collapse after his death. There is good reason to believe that since 1946 Stalin has been increasingly preoccupied with the future of the Soviet Union in the hands of his successors. And here again the party comes in. Stalin's personal position, with all its attached father-worship, can be bequeathed to no single individual; and this means that no matter what his views may be about the relative importance of Leninism and Russian nationalism, when he dies he must hand over to the party, or to his nominees in the name of the party, which must be in good heart to receive the trust. This is perhaps the most fundamentally important of all the reasons for the public return to Leninism. Stalin is in the position of a great man of business who has built up his firm, first by orthodox business methods, then by a total reliance on his own intuitions sustained by an inflexible will, intuitions often in direct contradiction to the accepted rules of business. He is aware of the inadequacy of those rules; but he knows he must leave his business in the hands of men who lack his genius. So, before he dies, he sets to work to put his firm on a proper and respectable footing.

This is what he is engaged in doing now, in circumstances hopelessly confused by the stresses of the Cold War. But all the time, behind the Leninist propaganda, the task of disengaging Great Russian patriotism from the trammels of Marxism, is quietly proceeding. The rewriting of history continues, and has entered a new phase. The idea of the great man is firmly established, never to be abandoned, and so is the idea of Soviet patriotism. But Stalin has moved far since the days when, to lash the people into further sacrifices, he stressed the traditional backwardness of Russia. The task of the historians now is twofold: instead of the history of prerevolutionary Russia being a single aspect of the dark night of suffering humanity, it has to be shown that Russia has always held a special, a unique place in the drama of mankind. It has to be shown that, in Stalin's favourite phrase, it was no accident that the revolution had come first to Russia. It came first to Russia because the Russians, since the beginning of time, had been first in everything, the guiding spirit of suffering humanity since its remote inauguration: the paraclete. And so it has been shown. Contemporary Stalinist historians have gone to all but unbelievable lengths to make out their case. Pankratova's *History of the U.S.S.R.* begins with the Assyrians and the Chaldeans, tracing the Russian people to the cradle of civilization on the grounds that the Mesopotamian cultures had branches in Transcaucasia, which is a part of the Soviet Union. The Varangian domination of Kiev Russia in the tenth century, which marked the beginning of Russia as a coherent idea, is shown as a trivial incident in the long and "progressive" history of the Eastern Slavs. The Scythians are presented as the blood ancestors of the contemporary Soviet citizen; and far from being a barbarian horde smashing down the antique cultures, they were the first liberators of the oppressed slave classes. Tsarist imperialism is explained away as not being imperialism at all, for the simple reason that conquest by a historically advanced power is not conquest but liberation. In the words of the ingenious Miss Pankratova, writing of one of the bloodiest episodes in the history of Russia, the subjection of Kazakhstan:

The drawing of Kazakhstan into the sphere of influence of a Russia which had already trodden the way of capitalist development, had a progressive influence on the further development of Kazakhstan.

This is the theme of the "White Man's Burden," translated into quasi-Marxist terms.

Again, even more ingeniously, the historian Abramson protests against the idea that the Khirgiz tribesmen were "conquered against their will." On the contrary: "By uniting with Russia the Khirgiz people came closer to the revolutionary elements of the Russian people, precisely at a time when the most revolutionary proletariat in the world, namely the Russian, appeared upon the stage of history." Even the conquest of superior cultures, as eighteenth-century Poland, is fitted into the general theory of liberation, on the grounds that even though the Poles may have been more culturally advanced than the Russians, their absorption into Russia was historically necessary at the time in order that Russia herself might freely devote her beneficent energies to liberating the backward peoples of Asia.

In fact, this last argument seems likely to be abandoned. Instead, it will shortly be denied that the Poles were, in fact, a superior culture. The most profitable occupation of the Soviet historians as I write is to antedate, sometimes by centuries, all the great crises of Russian development. For example, the beginning of feudalism among the Slavs has already been antedated to the sixth century, thus stealing a march on Western Europe; the period of enlightened absolutism has been put back from the time of Catherine and Frederick to the time of Peter. The beginning of capitalism has been put at the second decade of the eighteenth century, far in advance of Western capitalism. And, as this process continues, it becomes every day more easy to present Russian imperialism as a process of international protection.

The second task of the historians is to exalt the Great Russian people, the descendants of Muscovy, to a special place in the Soviet Union. It was Stalin again who gave the lead here at the Kremlin banquet to celebrate the victory over Hitler:

> Comrades, allow me to offer one more toast: the last. I drink to the health of our Soviet people and especially the Russian people. I drink especially to the health of the Russian people, because in this war it has proved itself the outstanding nation among all the nations belonging to the Soviet Union. I drink to the health of the Russian people because in this war it has earned universal recognition among all the peoples of our land as the leading power of the Soviet Union. I drink to the health of the Russian people not only because it has the qualities of leadership, but also because it has a clear understanding, a firm character, and endurance. The Russian people has believed in the correctness of its government's policy and it has sacrificed itself to bring about the downfall of Germany. This confidence of the Russian people in the Soviet government has proved to be the decisive force which brought victory over the historical enemy of mankind, over fascism. We thank the Russian people for this confidence! Good health to the Russian people!

That speech was made in the lovely white hall of St. George in the Kremlin, on May 24, 1945. It was made to a gathering of the elect of the Soviet Union. We do not know what the Ukrainians, the White Russians, the Cossacks, the Armenians, in the audience were feeling while Stalin spoke; but we guess. For this celebration of the dominant people of the U.S.S.R., the Great Russians, and their exaltation over all the other peoples of the Union, was an open return to the old Great Russian imperialism, with its queer messianic flavour, which we have discussed in an earlier chapter. It was also the formal statement of the negation, implicit for many years, of Stalin's own celebrated principles on the treatment of nationalities, which had won him Lenin's early regard. Stalin and his historians between them had thus set the stage for a more or less open return to a Great Russian expansionist policy which was nevertheless to be played down for the time being. Muscovy, with the aid of Marxist jargon, was to be able to justify itself as a liberating process at work throughout the world. Russia was the liberating force within the Soviet Union. The Soviet Union was the liberating force in the world as a whole.

I have already said enough to indicate that in Soviet practice the party line very frequently is deliberately allowed to lag behind Stalin's thinking. The Russian idea is not only very much in being, but it has also been modified and clarified, and the whole apparatus of party and police harnessed to it. The party, in a word, is now fully employed on a task which is in direct opposition to everything it nominally stands for. Stalin and, to a greater or lesser degree, Stalin's closer advisers, trained by Lenin to an acute perception of "internal contradictions," know this perfectly well; but the party as a whole does not yet know it. It has, however, been warned.

The warning was contained in the fantastic episode of the philologist, N. Y. Marr, in the course of which Stalin himself made a long, obscure, and extraordinary pronouncement, ostensibly about philological studies, which will, I believe, prove to have the same sort of radical significance for the next decade (and longer) as the slogan "Socialism in One Country" had for the thirties. The episode occurred on the eve of the Korean war, and was immediately eclipsed, as far as the outer world was concerned, by news from the battlefronts at Lake Success and on the 38th Parallel. But it was not eclipsed in Russia; and its consequences may, in the long run, be more important than a dozen unfortunate Koreas. It must, therefore, have a chapter to itself.

5

The Amazing Episode of N. Y. Marr

PROFESSOR N. Y. MARR, WHO DIED IN 1934, was the son of a
Scottish father and a Georgian mother. He was one of the
most esteemed scholars of the Soviet Union and its greatest philologist. Until the summer of 1950 his memory was
held in reverence and his theory of language had since the
war been celebrated as one of the cornerstones of Soviet
scientific teaching. It came in particularly useful in the
great struggle against "formalism" in the arts and sciences
and in support of the new Soviet idea of achieving mas-
tery of the very laws of nature, an idea best symbolized by
Academician Lysenko's biological theories, which denied
the existence of immutable hereditary characteristics and
insisted that new species could be bred under special conditions of culture and environment. In terms of conventional Marxist categories, language, according to Marr, was
an element of the superstructure of society, which changed
as society changed, being the product, like the political,
legal, religious, artistic, and philosophical elements of a

given society, of the ruling class of the moment. From this it followed that language under a Socialist society would change, and, under a Socialist society embracing the whole world, would develop into a world-wide language. It was this conviction, incidentally, which lay behind the immense fertility of invention in the creation of artificial words which distinguished the early days of Bolshevism. Marr himself had written: "In this moment of revolutionary creativeness it is altogether too absurd to speak of reforming the alphabet and grammar of the Russian language. . . . It is not at all a question of reform. It is a question of a radical change in our habits of speech, a switching of the language itself on to a new line leading to a true mass-language. What is wanted is not a form, nor a reform, or new wine in old bottles. What is wanted is a new scaffold which will carry a new structure of language valid not only for the whole Soviet Union but also for the whole world." Stalin also had expressed himself categorically in this sense at the Sixteenth Party Congress, where he spoke of the merging of all languages into one common language. So Professor Marr had the highest possible support. Until suddenly everything was changed.

There was a premonitory rumble on May 19, 1950, when, for no apparent reason, *Pravda* came out with an enlarged edition announcing that the question of Soviet philology had become a burning one which could no longer be staved off, and containing a long and tedious discussion by various authorities about philology in general and Professor Marr in particular. The explosion followed on June 20, when all Russia woke up to find exactly half their copy of *Pravda* filled with a closely printed letter by Stalin himself on a subject most of them had never heard of (for few had read the academic discussion of May 9): Professor Marr, or, as Stalin called him, N. Y. Marr, and

his philological theory. There were ten thousand words of
it, or material for a two-hour lecture. Nine thousand words
said nothing at all; but the remaining thousand presaged a
revolution in Soviet development. After this major broad-
side Stalin came back again in a series of "answers" to in-
quiring young comrades, and in one of these "answers" the
nature of this revolution was formally stated.

The impact of this episode on the Soviet intellectuals
was immense. As far as the ordinary Russian was concerned, he had no idea at all of what it was all about, except that it was epoch-making. It was obviously epoch-
making because this was the first time Stalin had broken
silence in four years, apart from a few written replies to
foreign journalists about war and peace and American
slumps and the possibilities of coexistence, all designed
quite evidently to keep the international ball in play and
for no other purpose. This was something different. Stalin,
under cover of this obscure philological debate, was saying
something tremendous, but nobody knew what it was.

He said a number of incidental things, which put the
leaders of Soviet thought into a panic. He attacked the
"antiformalism" of Professor Marr, which alarmed writers
and scientists who had built up their whole careers on the
antiformalist line of Zhdanov and Lysenko and filled with
despondency those who did not care but at least thought
they knew where they stood. He attacked the highhanded
line taken by Marr's disciples, criticizing their "Arakcheyev
régime" in words which any foreign scientists might use
about Soviet science in general—and which all Soviet intellectuals in every sphere were bound to apply to themselves.
But all this was a sideline. The main object of the letter
was to prepare the ground for a formal announcement of
the relativity of Marxism. Stalin stopped short of that in
this first extraordinary document, which he devoted mainly

to proving and demonstrating the falseness of Marr's conception of language as part of the superstructure of society, and therefore liable to radical changes. It was, he asserted, a part of the base, and therefore a constant. Only the most acute could have seen the next advance from that position. Stalin dropped certain hints. He wrote in the best of good humour, playing the rôle of the kindly uncle with a twinkle in his eye, as never before. "I have been asked," he started off, "by a group of comrades of the younger generation to say in the press what I think about certain questions of philology, and particularly with regard to Marxism in philology. I am no philologist myself, and of course I cannot tell the comrades everything they want to know. But when it comes to the question of Marxism in philology—well, I myself am directly mixed up in that; and so I have agreed to answer a number of the comrades' questions. . . ."

It is in this tone of voice that he approaches the fringe of his real purpose, halfway through his argument, when he makes fun of so-called Marxists who cling too rigidly to the letter of the book:

> We had "Marxists" at one time who used to say that the railways left in our country after the October Revolution were bourgeois productions, and that therefore it was improper for us, as Marxists, to go on using them. They had to be torn up and new "proletarian" railways built in their place. We nicknamed those people the "Troglodytes."

And in a discussion as to whether progress in society was made by sudden leaps or explosions, as Marx had taught, with his ideas of violent revolution, or in a continuous curve, he prepared his readers for the conception that all things were relative, even Karl Marx:

It should be said, in general, for the benefit of all comrades who have a weakness for explosions, that the law of
transition from an old category to a new by means of an
explosion is not only inapplicable to the history of the
development of languages; it is also by no means always
applicable to other social phenomena of a basic or super-
structural character. It is compulsory for a society
divided into hostile classes. But it is not at all compulsory
for a society which has no hostile classes.

Nevertheless, the general impression made by this monumental contribution to *Pravda's* correspondence columns
was one of mystery. Stalin was starting something, but
precisely what, it was impossible to say. That he was forti-
fying earlier observations on the particular value of the
Russian people and the Russian heritage was perfectly
clear: the most obvious theme emerging from his letter was
that the Russian language belonged to all time and would
not be corrupted in the interests of a hypothetical world
language. And, bearing in mind Stalin's previous exaltation of the Russian people, it would be safe to deduce
that he was now calling for the restoration of the Russian
language as the common language of the Soviet Union.
In fact, this was in accord with recent tendencies in the
various republics, where, on one pretext or another, Russian was being used increasingly as the teaching language
in the schools. It was also clear that Stalin was worried by
the extreme rigidity with which, after the Zhdanov purge
of the arts and the Lysenko purge of the sciences, the new
line was being pursued among the intellectuals, largely
stultifying the work of some of the most gifted men in
Russia. But, with the best will in the world, a short lesson
in the permanence of the Russian language and an attack
on the new sycophancy in the sciences did not call for this

colossal apparatus of quasi-Marxist exegesis. Thus the letter of June 20 created a panic and a ferment and left a doubt.

The doubt was not immediately resolved. But ten days later Stalin returned to his theme, this time in the columns of *Bolshevik,* the party fortnightly, in which the party line is customarily announced in its pristine subtlety and delicacy before it is popularized by *Pravda* for the masses. Still playing at being a jolly uncle, Stalin came forward with a long letter to a member of the younger generation, mentioned this time by name: Comrade Krasheninnovka, a young woman. But what he said added very little. It was not until a month later that the issue of *Bolshevik* for the second fortnight of July revealed what it was all about. This time there were three separate answers to three letters of inquiry, and the critical one was the last.

"Dear Comrade Sanzheyev," the series started, in higher spirits than ever, "I am answering your letter after a very long delay because it was only yesterday that your letter was produced to me by the office of the Central Committee . . ." Comrade Sanzheyev, the most astonished young man in Russia, received a kind, wise lecture from the great man who could wink at him from the fastnesses of the Kremlin about the office red tape of the holy of holies. Comrades Belkin and Furer, in the next letter, had a sharp and donnish rebuke, to show that the great man, much as he loved his pupils, would certainly stand no nonsense:

Comrades D. Belkin and S. Furer! I have received your letters. Your error consists in confusing two different things and substituting for the subject which I examined in my letter to Comrade Krasheninnovka quite a different subject. . . . In that reply I deal with normal people who possess language. . . . You substitute anomalous, languageless people, deaf-mutes, who have no language. . . . As you see, this is an entirely different subject, to which I did not refer and could not refer, because philology studies normal people who possess a language and not anomalous deaf-mutes who have no language. . . . Evidently you are interested in deaf-mutes first and only afterwards in questions of philology. No doubt it was this interest which prompted you to ask me a number of questions. Very well, if you insist, I have nothing against meeting your wish. . . . And so, how do things stand with deaf-mutes? Do they think? Do thoughts arise? Yes, they think; thoughts do arise. . . .

And so on. I could not resist printing that rather long extract, although it is quite irrelevant to our argument, because the world is not often treated to the spectacle of Stalin at play. The play, of course, was wholly calculated. Immediately after this deliberate nonsense, and without the least warning or emphasis, comes another letter, this time to a Comrade Kholopov, who receives the whole works, as the saying goes. The purpose of this extraordinary performance is at last made clear:

"Comrade A. Kholopov. I have received your letter. I am rather late in replying owing to pressure of work," he starts off, and then proceeds straight to the heart of the matter with a drive and crispness and decision of articulation which is entirely alien to his normal lecturing style, though still turgid enough by non-Soviet standards. I quote the opening paragraphs in full because this pronouncement has passed unnoticed by the West and yet contains, I believe, the key not only to Stalin's thinking, but to the future of Soviet Russia:

Your letter tacitly proceeds from two assumptions: the assumption that it is permissible to quote the works of an author separated from the historical period to which the quotation refers; and secondly, the assumption that this or that conclusion or formula of Marxism, arrived at as a result of the study of one period of historical development, is correct for all periods of development and hence must remain unalterable.

I must say that both these assumptions are profoundly wrong.

Let me give a few examples.

1. In the forties of the last century when there was still no monopoly capitalism, when capitalism was developing more or less smoothly along an ascending line, spreading to new territories which it had not yet occupied, so that the law of uneven development could not yet operate with its full force, Marx and Engels came to the conclusion that the socialist revolution could not win in one country alone but only as a result of a general blow in all, or in the most civilized, countries. This conclusion then became a guiding precept for Marxists.

However, at the beginning of the twentieth century, especially in the period of the First World War, when it became clear to all that premonopoly capitalism had obviously developed into monopoly capitalism, when ascending capitalism had become declining capitalism, when war brought to light the incurable weaknesses of the world imperialist front so that the law of uneven development now predetermined the maturing of the proletarian revolution in different countries at different times, Lenin, proceeding from the Marxist theory, came to the conclusion that in the new conditions of development the socialist revolution could triumph fully in one country, taken separately, that the simultaneous victory of the socialist revolution in all countries or most of the civilized countries was impossible in view of the unevenness of the maturing of the revolution in these countries, that the old formula of Marx and Engels no longer corresponded to the new historical conditions.

As can be seen, we have here two different conclusions on the problem of the victory of socialism, which not only contradict one another but even exclude one another.

Thus dogmatists and pedants who, without delving into the substance of the matter, cite quotations formally, isolated from the historical conditions, may say that one of these conclusions must be discarded as absolutely incorrect while the other conclusion, as absolutely correct, must be applied to all periods of development. But Marxists cannot but know that these dogmatists and pedants are wrong; they cannot but know that both conclusions are correct, *although not absolutely, but each for its own time:* the conclusion of Marx and Engels for the period of premonopoly capitalism and the conclusion of Lenin for the period of monopoly capitalism. . . .

After that the letter tails off. Stalin uses his new approach first to show that the celebrated doctrine of the withering away' of the state as expounded by Engels in *Anti-Dühring* was correct for that epoch but incorrect for the present epoch marked by the "capitalist encirclement" of a single Socialist country; secondly, to explain his own change of attitude about a universal language, which brings the argument back to its starting point. But the crux of the whole affair has nothing to do essentially with poor Professor Marr. It has to do with the relativity of Marxism, as expressed in the opening passage quoted above and in the concluding paragraphs:

Dogmatists and pedants regard Marxism, the separate conclusions and formulæ of Marxism, as a collection of dogmas which "never" change, notwithstanding the changes in the conditions of the development of society. They think that if they learn these conclusions and formulæ by heart and start quoting them without rhyme or reason they will be able to solve all problems, in the expectation that such conclusions and formulæ learnt by heart will be applicable in all times and all countries and for every occasion in life. But the sort of people who can think like this are those who see only the letter of Marxism without being aware of its substance, and who learn by rote texts of Marxist conclusions and formulæ and do not understand their content.

Marxism is the science of the laws of development of nature and society, the science of the revolution of the oppressed and exploited masses, the science of the victory of socialism in all countries, the science of building Communist society. Marxism as a science cannot stand in one place, it develops and is being perfected. In its development Marxism cannot fail to be enriched by new experience, by new knowledge—consequently its separate formulæ and conclusions cannot fail to change with the course of time, cannot fail to be replaced by new formulæ and conclusions corresponding to the new historical tasks. Marxism does not recognize immutable conclusions and formulæ, binding for all epochs and periods. Marxism is the enemy of all dogmatism.

J. Stalin, July 28, 1950.

Marxism is what you think it is. Marxism is what you need it to be. Socialism is what Soviet society is. Communism is what it will be. This, in effect, is Stalin's great legacy to his successors; and by a neat distortion of the truth he has fastened "Socialism in One Country" on to Lenin and so brought Lenin into the process as a precedent. And the occasion for the whole revelation is the discovery that language is an unchanging constant, at least in "the epoch before the victory of socialism on a world scale." The language Stalin is talking about is the language of Great Russia.

Is this all a part of the master plan?

6

Internal Contradictions

THE DEVELOPMENT OUTLINED in the preceding chapter, when translated into terms of Soviet foreign policy, faces us with the most interesting situation it is possible to imagine. In the person of one remarkable man we see, on the one hand, an autocrat of a great and victorious power publicly glorifying a Soviet fatherland led by the dominant Great Russians and drawing its inspiration from the ancient despotic and imperial traditions of the tsars; on the other, the obscure figure of the general secretary of the All-Union Communist Party, ostensibly basing all his activity on a historical theory which denies the validity of great men, privileged nations, and historical tradition and sets as its ultimate ideal the coming of the proletarian revolution all over the world.

Besides being interesting, it is a situation of extreme complexity, and if we ourselves fail to unravel it to our own satisfaction, there is at least some comfort in the thought that Stalin and his friends must be equally at sea.

One thing is absolutely clear: while it is a gross over-simplification to speak of Stalin's foreign policy as a simple reversion to the old tsarist imperialism, it is still more wide of the mark to speak of it exclusively in terms of the Marxist-Leninist struggle for world revolution and to cite all the statements in *Problems of Leninism* and *A Short History of the Communist Party,* as though these publications formed a sort of Muscovite *Mein Kampf.* This is the fashionable view of the moment, propagated by earnest politicians who have never read either, and who talk about Stalin as a would-be world conqueror as though world conquest was the most natural thing in the world instead of something unheard of and absurd. We, and particularly the Americans, are here the victims of our own wartime propaganda when, for the sake of effect, we spoke of Hitler as a seeker after world dominion, knowing that in fact he was nothing of the kind. We shall have to say more about world conquest and the false analogy between Stalin and Hitler, which has led us into such dire straits, when we come to consider the future. But now we are still in the present, and making the point that nothing could be more erroneous than to suppose that Stalin tenaciously believes in everything he has ever said and written about the proletarian revolution. If this book does nothing else but make that much clear, it will have served its purpose. But it is one thing to say that Stalin does not believe in everything he has said, and to show the contradictions in his attitude, and quite another to decide what, in the end, he really does believe. To get to grips with that problem we must attack our subject from another angle. We must consider what Stalin is actually doing now in his conflict with the West; we must consider the nature of communism outside Russia, which is far more important to Stalin than the nature of communism inside Russia; and we must form an image of the Soviet reality, which Stalin and his colleagues are faced with each day of their lives.

But we can approach these matters with a clear head only if we abandon the idea of a grand Bolshevik design, patiently and deliberately worked out over a period of thirty years. No man, no government, in the history of the world, has been capable of a tenth part of the foresight attributed to Stalin and his friends by those who, without a shred of hard evidence, insist that Stalin is working for world conquest. If a man of Stalin's highly practical nature ever allows himself time off for daydreaming in the intervals of his infinitely arduous task of preserving his own skin and his country's identity, he may sometimes dream of a Moscow-dominated planet; but he also knows very well that this consummation is not for him, and when he wakes up he must return to the daily chore of keeping Stalinist Russia on the map at all. Indeed, if Stalin and his unlikable friends were a tenth as able as they are usually made out to be, then we should really have no business to be struggling against them: such paragons should be begged to rule the world. But they are not paragons. They are opportunist statesmen of great ability and perfect unscrupulousness, manœuvring for advantage in a conscienceless sort of way, improvising from day to day and year to year within a general historical conception which has about as much relevance to our daily lives as a belief in Judgment Day. They are engaged in a ruthless and unremitting struggle with the Russian people, whose most deeply rooted characteristics, even in those who think of themselves as model Communists, are hopelessly at odds with the conception of a modern, closely organized, and industrialized state. They are also engaged, as Stalin sees it, in a ruthless and unremitting struggle with the "capitalist encirclement," which, willy-nilly, is committed to a struggle to the death with the base and headquarters of the world revolution—so long as the world revolution is still preached. Every day in half a hundred different ways Stalin and his friends are faced with the task of reconciling the demands of their long-term objectives with the day-to-day survival of the Soviet Union. They do not always succeed in this task. Now, for example, they find themselves committed to contradictory policies, such as seeking trade with the West while simultaneously sabotaging Western production, or such as supplying with oil and warlike stores the military machine which, next year, is going to batter down their barricades. Since the war, from one point of view, the short-term needs and the long-term policies may seem to have been working fairly merrily together; but even this is largely an illusion. And the time may come at any minute when, as more than once before, the loyal servants of Moscow throughout the world must be thrown to the wolves to keep the Soviet Union on its feet.

3. The Cold War

1

Domestic Background

J UST AS IT IS HARDLY AN EXAGGERATION to say that the history of the past thirty years in Russia has been the history of the struggle between doctrinaire Leninism and the Russian reality, so it is equally true to say that Soviet foreign policy has been very much a reflection of the domestic situation. Thus, before we turn to the so-called Cold War, we should first glance at the state of Russia as it appeared to a sympathetic observer on the eve of that war, which broke out, as I understand it, in the summer of 1947. Of course, if we take the Marxism of Stalin at its face value, we must date the outbreak of the Cold War to that autumn day in 1917 when Lenin assumed control in Petrograd, and this is what an extremely articulate school of thought would like us to do. But, for reasons which by now should be clear enough, I do not think we are justified in taking Stalin's Marxism at its face value. Further, even if we believe, as I do not, that there has been a continuous and persistent progression in a predetermined direction ever since the revolution, what we mean by the Cold War is the specific campaign aimed at the ultimate disruption of the West. My own date is the summer of 1947.

It is not easy nowadays to recapture the Russian reality which underlies the propaganda barrages from both sides. Because of this I offer, just as it was written at the time, at the critical moment a month or two before Stalin decided to open his grand offensive against the West, a chapter of impressions derived from a visit to Russia in the spring of that year. It was the first time I had seen Russia since 1943, just after Stalingrad; and it was during this visit that, after the failure of the Moscow Conference of Foreign Ministers, Russia's relations with the West had fallen into a deadlock, which was soon to be broken by the impact of the Marshall Plan. This, then, is how it seemed to me then:

The three most striking facts about Soviet Russia today are elementary ones which confront one wherever one goes: they are the need, the discipline, and the fear. I shall consider them in that order. But there is another primary fact of quite a different kind, and all-important. It is quite a remarkable fact in itself: the fact of the continued survival of the U.S.S.R. It is, indeed, a recurrent miracle. So long as we inhabit a world of sovereign nations and power politics, so long, that is to say, as the first duty of all statesmen is to preseve the coherence, integrity, and independence of their own countries, we have to admit that any régime which contrives to hold together the hopelessly fluid and anarchical people of the Russian plain (to say nothing of the great Russian Empire) has fulfilled its first duty in face of the heaviest odds and, therefore, justified itself. I question whether any régime but the existing

Stalin régime could have held Russia together in the fight against Germany and emerged with the Russian Empire not only intact but also enlarged. This does not mean that the Russian people, in peacetime, might not be a great deal happier under a different régime. Left to themselves, indeed, they would almost certainly have broken up into innumerable small and fairly primitive communities. They would, in a word, have ceased to be citizens of the U.S.S.R. And by now they would have been swallowed up by Germany and Japan. The price they pay for being the citizens of an independent nation is Marshal Stalin. It is a formidable price, but it has its compensations. And it is emphatically not the first duty of a statesman in this current phase of world society to ask whether his people would be happier and better off under an alien government. The sovereign nation is still the order of the day, and until this ceases to be so the statesman who puts anything above the survival of the nation he rules quite simply betrays his trust. If we do not like that we had better start arranging things differently. Stalin held the Russian people together and forced them to arm themselves at the cost of inconceivable suffering. Nobody else, I believe, would have proved sufficiently hard and ruthless and single-minded to pay, or force others to pay, the necessary price. It is only possible to appreciate the magnitude of his achievement, for better or for worse, if we know something about the nature of the Russian people and if we consider our three salient facts of life in Russia today: the need, the discipline, and the fear.

I shall deal first with the need. It is useless to think of Russia today otherwise than in terms of desperate, to us inconceivable, hard-upness. I am not discussing standards of living. (Far too much fuss has been made in the past about the grimness and poverty of life in Russia—grim and threadbare enough by our standards it always has been since the revolution, but not, except in periods of acute crisis, by Russian standards, the standards, that is, of the Russian masses.) I mean rather the destitution caused directly by the late war, in part by the impact of the war itself, in part by the government's preparations for it. And this is overwhelming.

People tell me they are sick and tired of hearing about the sufferings of Russia in the war, of the millions of dead men and women and of the wholesale devastation. But, in fact, they have scarcely begun to hear of them. They know, as an abstraction, that between ten and twenty million people died. They know, again as an abstraction, that the Germans destroyed everything that stood in their way as they retreated. But they do not seem to know even as an abstraction, most of them, that six hundred thousand people died of starvation during the siege of Leningrad and that the corpses, which could not be buried in winter, were kept indoors, the deaths not registered, so that the survivors could go on drawing the rations of the dead, when there were any to draw. They do not seem to know that the people of Moscow during the winters of 1941 and 1942 lived without heat and without light and without gas for cooking for weeks on end, on virtually nothing but black bread—not primitive peasants, but highly cultivated human beings working with their brains. And they do not seem to know that German destructiveness did not consist merely in blowing up factories and power stations and locomotives and tractors, but was carried down to the last detail—so that all the way from Mozhaisk to Smolensk, for example, every single telegraph pole along that interminable railway line, itself torn up, had been chopped down six inches from the ground, and wheelbarrows were destroyed and removed with as single-minded a passion as five-ton trucks and tractors. They do not seem to know that the present shortage of tractors, horses, and cows to pull the ploughs, which themselves no longer exist, is such that a most familiar sight in the spring of this year (1947) was to see twenty or thirty peasant women turning the soil of a hundred-acre field with spades and dibbing in potatoes as they went.

And even if we do know these things theoretically, they have not been grasped. Because if we had grasped these simple human facts we should not spend so much time wondering what the Russians mean by, for example, their impossible demands for reparations. We should know that what they above all mean is, quite simply, reparations. And we should not wonder why the Russians are occupying so much of Europe; we should know that the Russians are there in the first place to lay hold of everything they can move back to Russia. All under pressure of this appalling need.

It is not enough to exclaim that this is a shortsighted policy, and, as it were, wave it off the map. Of course it is shortsighted. I have no doubt that the men in the Kremlin know this as well as anyone. It is shortsighted to sell valued possessions at a loss to satisfy an immediate need. It is shortsighted to borrow at exorbitant interest. But the knowledge of this does not do away with the need. And there are times when men have had to borrow at exorbitant interest or die then and there. Most of them have borrowed and hoped for something to turn up before the interest fell due. Russia has grabbed all she can and has tried to grab more, the first supreme and urgent need being to keep the Russian people on their feet from day to day *now*.

The Russian government itself is largely responsible for the failure of the Western nations to realize the intensity of Russia's need. During the war it laboured ruthlessly to conceal the true conditions of life, as, for example, the Leningrad famine, for fear of giving encouragement and comfort to the Germans. Since the war, except when the demand for reparations has been directly in question, as at the Moscow Conference, it has laboured even more ruthlessly to conceal the true conditions of life in order to hide Russia's temporary weakness from the rest of the world, particularly from Great Britain and the United States. That may be called a shortsighted policy too. But the appearance of immediate strength, built up at infinite cost in human suffering, has nevertheless enabled the Kremlin to get its way in Eastern Europe, upon which it set great store.

The need is universal, and it covers almost everything. As the people feel it, the priorities would probably be in this order: food (food above all), clothing, housing, rest, consumer goods other than clothing, communal amenities, transport. But, as the government sees it, the priorities are more like this, or were until a few months ago: heavy industry (which is, of course, not a popular need at all, although its improvement is necessary for the satisfaction of some popular needs, as well as for other things, such as tanks); food (which means agriculture); communal amenities, housing, transport, consumer goods, including clothing, and finally, after a long interval, rest. The conflict between these two lists of priorities is a reflection of the conflict between the people and the government of Russia. . . . So long as the discrepancy between the government's list and the people's list is as acute as it is today, the ideal unity of government and people will not be achieved.

This does not mean the prospect of popular revolt, or anything like it. It simply means that there will be frequent discontent, some demoralization, and a great deal of instinctive ca'canny—which is the Soviet equivalent of absenteeism. The main reason for the, to our eyes, curious emphasis on communal amenities is quite simple; it is not in fact at all curious. We have a housing shortage in Britain, but that does not mean that we turn theatres and cinemas into blocks of flats. It does not even stop us putting up more cinemas. The Russian housing shortage is appalling— in the cities it was intolerable before the war, and it has now been magnified to the point where Moscow has about five million people, a million of them unregistered, living in houses for two million; while the countryside—all the countryside west of Moscow and Stalingrad—is now in even worse condition, with families by tens of thousands living in holes in rubble, or large dugouts roofed with earth. The Russian forests in the north could provide all the timber required; but there is neither the machinery to cut and shape the trees nor the transport to bring them where they are wanted. In face of this shortage, the only immediate course to adopt is to use the available material on magnificent communal centres which take people's minds off their own troubles and at the same time stimulate their sense of pride. So this is done. In the case of a city like Stalingrad, the first thing is to rebuild the factories, the people housing themselves in the rubble as best they may; the second thing is to put a bit of colour into the lives of these modern cave dwellers; and a new communal centre can provide this with less trouble and effort than would be required to rebuild a single street of apartment houses. So the houses come later.

The drought in the summer of 1946 was for a long time concealed. But it was finally hinted at as the reason for the continued existence of bread rationing by Zhdanov on the occasion of the 1946 anniversary of the October

Revolution. In January 1947 it was officially declared to have been the most serious drought since 1891, which was the year of the greatest famine. Even the 1921 drought was not so intensive and extensive. But the 1891 and 1921 famines have not been repeated because, in spite of the ravages of war, the Soviet economy has proved sufficiently strong, flexible, and well developed to stand the strain— just. There was a good harvest east of the Urals, above all in Altai and Kazakhstan, where in tsarist days there was no developed agriculture; and somehow the communication system, immensely developed under Kaganovich but stricken by the war, managed to function adequately. Even so, there were terrible times in the Ukraine, and all through the Black Earth belt to Saratov on the Volga. In Rumania the same drought led to stark famine. As far as one can make out, there has not been stark famine in any of the Russian lands. People are ill and unable to work for lack of food in certain areas. Industrial and agricultural output has fallen accordingly. The bread ration for White Russia and the Ukraine is something like 250 grammes a day, against 550 for an able-bodied worker elsewhere in Russia. That is the barest subsistence ration, when bread is the only solid food, and you can do no work on it. If it had not been for U.N.R.R.A., which is now being dissolved, and certain Soviet improvements in transport and agriculture referred to above, it would have resulted in nothing less than famine. As it is, it has to be recorded that, for the first time in history, a government of Russia has succeeded in preventing a first-class drought from killing millions. This is the sort of thing the Communist Party of the Soviet Union has always said it would do, and it seems to be doing it.

The effect of this natural calamity in the first year of peace on the rest of Russia, and notably Moscow, has been most marked. The continuation of bread rationing was a bitter disappointment. The increase in price of off-the-ration foods in the new so-called commercial shops threw millions back on their barely sufficient rations and caused millions more to take on extra work for roubles with which to buy food. What one might call the white-collar class in the cities is killing itself with overwork; and when it has bought the extra food it has no money over for such clothes as there are. It is a common thing to find a man doing three separate jobs. The main trouble is that legitimate dependents simply do not get enough to keep them alive. By legitimate dependents I mean semi-invalids, grandparents, etc. Their ration is not intended to drive them to work; but they get barely enough to keep body and soul together in repose. By illegitimate dependents I mean wives without children, or with children over ten. These are not recognized as dependents. They are driven to work, or to be wholly parasitic on their husbands, by the simple means of withholding all food. "He who shall not work, neither shall he eat," in the quasi-Biblical phrase of the Stalin constitution. They receive a ration card entitling them each week to one box of matches and one packet of salt. Nothing else. So unless their parents or husbands can support them off the ration—on potatoes at 20 roubles a kilo, and bread at 10 roubles a slice, and meat at 450 roubles a kilo—they have to go to work too.

In a word, most Russians in the cities just now feel they are worse off than ever before. It is a feeling that we in Britain sometimes have, and, like ours, it is illusory. They are a great deal better off than they were in 1942 and 1943, but nothing like so well off as in 1944 and 1945, when life began to brighten a good deal. The recent decline is above all due to the drought, but partly also to the exhaustion of those consumer goods that came from Rus-

sian-occupied countries. These do not last forever. On the
other hand, if there is a good harvest this year, as at present promises, and if the Russian government does not
starve its own people by exporting too much grain to
Britain, to France, or to Eastern Europe in pursuance
of a carefully calculated foreign policy, people will feel a
great deal better this time next year and life will be more
cheerful again.

It will have been gathered that the drought and German
wickedness are not the only things responsible for the present extreme shortage of the things the Russian people
want, from food downwards. The other responsible agent is
the Soviet government itself. I mentioned heavy industry
as number one priority. Heavy industry, and notably the
production of steel, has to be built up to make machines
for light industry; but not on the scale at present under-
taken. Heavy industry is also required for making armaments, and large sums of money and tremendous efforts
are being devoted to this barren purpose, increasing the
present distress of the Russian people accordingly. Further,
there is an immense expenditure of manpower and material on the creation of new centres in the fastnesses of
Siberia, material and manpower which is thus diverted
from the restoration of the old centres in the Ukraine. The
motive here is also military. It is beyond my scope to discuss Russia's warlike preparations and their implications
for the future of the world. I mention them only in connection with the need of the Russian people, which is, as
we have seen, the result partly of German destructiveness,
partly of a natural calamity, and partly of the Kremlin's
obsession, for whatever reason, with Soviet power and war
potential.

The present acute need, it must be remembered, is
superimposed upon an age-old poverty, which was reduced

to destitution by the revolution; after twenty-five years of sacrificial toil, the people were winning through to slight but real alleviation just when Hitler attacked and threw everything back—but not, which is the remarkable thing, to chaos. Some of the correspondents with me in Moscow for the Conference in April 1947 mistook the monuments of this centuries-old need for signs of decay beneath the present régime. It is important not to make this mistake. Quite apart from being unfair to the new Russia, it leads one to believe that the Soviet Union is weaker than it really is. I have spent a good deal of time in the last two years trying to persuade people that Russia is nothing like the iron monster of the popular imagination. But now the pendulum is swinging too far in the other direction. Russia is nothing like so strong as she looks from a distance, but she is a very great deal stronger than she looks from close, too. Most of us would think it the end of all things if we had to go home from our work to a dugout. The Russian hates it, but for him it is very far from the end.

I have dealt at particular length with the need because that gives the background against which the other points, the discipline and the fear, are thrown up.

By discipline I mean particularly party discipline. For nearly a year now a fairly continuous purge has been going on in Russia, and particularly, of course, in the Ukraine, where the collective system for agriculture broke down during the war. But it has been a very mild purge. Instead of being liquidated, as on past occasions, offenders are more usually reprimanded, sent away on some unpleasant assignment for a few months, and then brought back again into their own line of business. I met two or three men who had only recently been disgraced, but who were back at their own work as though nothing had happened. The full weight of the purge has been felt within the party itself; and its aim seems to have been partly to restore the party discipline, which had got a little ragged during the war; partly to reduce the party numbers, which had become swollen to something like seven millions during the war—deliberately and for a special purpose; and partly to eliminate certain opposition elements and thus to prepare for the next so long delayed party congress, at which a good deal of criticism could well be expected. All that refers to the cleaning up of the party itself. Outside the party, the main object of the purge has been to strengthen the position of the party in the country and to stop certain tendencies deliberately encouraged during the war—for instance, the glorification of the army and the glorification of the Russian tradition as opposed to the Soviet tradition.

All this was only to be expected. But what is interesting and new is the extreme mildness of the purge, and the fact that the Kremlin's bark has been very much worse than its bite. Offenders are spoken to more in sorrow than in anger. And, in a word, there is a deliberate and widespread effort to present Stalin as a stern but understanding father, instead of as a jealous god. You see this reflected in the Russian theatre, which, by and large, is in a very poor state just now. It is the day of the little man, of difficult choices, of gallant striving after the good. One of the most popular plays in Moscow—I forget its title—is about a young woman who has to choose between a dashing young Red Army hero and a rather dim young engineer who worked without glory during the war. At first the soldier has it all his own way; but in the end, to great applause, the young technician wins out. The heroine has done the right thing. Of course, we knew she would: our Soviet young women can always be relied on to do the right thing. That is the atmosphere. But the dashing young hero, so recently the most fêted man in the world, does not quite know whether he is coming or going. This paternalism is also reflected in the recent abolition of the death penalty, in the emphasis on the watchdog character —a watchdog for the people, of course—of the public prosecutor's office, and in the promise of some sort of *habeas corpus*.

The immediate aim behind this development—and this brings me to my next point, the fear—is, I think, twofold. The obvious aim is to reassure people and give them a renewed sense of security: to do away with fear. The longer-term aim, which is more controversial, is, I believe, to prepare the country for a disengaging action, which is now taking place, a withdrawal all along the line, a turning inwards and away from the corrupt and tainted Western world in the traditional Russian manner. I cannot develop this thesis now: it has more to do with Soviet foreign policy than with the impressions gathered on a short return visit to Moscow. It is a matter easier to study outside than inside Russia. But I had better put it on record, if only as a pointer to the new paternalism and parochialism (it is very far from new in principle) which is noticeable in Russia today, that what I believe the main line of Russian foreign policy to be is, precisely, a concealed withdrawal, a retreat without loss of face. Stalin has taken all he can out of Europe, and he is now getting out under cover of a noisy rearguard action. We shall hear less and less of Russia in Europe, and more and more of communism—and the two are not necessarily synonyms.

There are three kinds of fear in Russia today. There is the fear in the Kremlin of external attack, which is partly doctrinal and party pathological. Tied up with this, of course, is the Kremlin's fear of internal breakdown, caused not by revolt, but by the nonfulfilment of the Plans owing to voluntary or involuntary feebleness of effort on the part of the people. Then there is the fear in the hearts of the people themselves, which is twofold, internal and external. There is nothing new about the fear of the M.V.D., the fear of the jealous god, which Stalin is now trying to replace with healthy respect for the heavy father; he will not do that in a day, and meanwhile the fear remains. But the second sort of fear is quite new. It is fear of war at any moment. The Russian people do not like war, they have never liked it, they have had a great deal of it. Russian women when they hear of a great victory do not rejoice: they weep—because a victory means casualties. They are now, or they were a month or two ago, going about in deadly fear that war may break out tomorrow. "How is the conference going? Is it to be war or peace?" You heard that pathetic, urgent question on every side, wherever you went. It sounds unbelievable, but it is true. And the people have their government to thank for this fear. The government is afraid of war too; but not of immediate war. They are afraid of war sometime in the next twenty years, before they are ready for it. But this fear, which a year ago they deliberately instilled into the people, and are now trying hard to remove, is something quite different. It was artificial and calculated propaganda, which miscarried. In order to keep the workers and the peasants up to scratch, and to excuse themselves for making the people go without for still longer, they manufactured an artificial war scare—so successfully that instead of stimulating the people to further effort it had a paralysing effect. This was really too much. After all the years of rewardless toil, after winning the greatest war in history, to be faced with a new war then and there—it was not worth it. And so the government has to back-pedal: Stalin makes reassuring statements to visiting journalists; and the death penalty is abolished because an era of settled peace lies ahead—that sort of thing. It will be some time before this new line begins to take effect. Meanwhile the people are hungry, weary, starved of colour, bewildered, and desperately afraid.

And meanwhile the Kremlin goes on with its appalling self-appointed task of achieving production parity with the United States, with, when this year's harvest is in, steel once more as the first priority—and, while it does this, of turning Russia into a fortress, consolidating what it can of its external gains, setting up obedient governments before evacuating countries that it cannot hold, and using foreign Communist Parties and national jealousies to keep the rest of the world as weak as possible by creating division and fratricidal strife.

2

Declaration of War

I T SEEMS TO ME that those impressions, recorded about
four years ago, in the spring of 1947, have an actuality
which it would be hard, if not impossible, to recapture today; and they certainly have their place in the story now
unfolding. The facts, as far as they went, were as reported;
but they did not go far enough. As we have already seen,
Russian casualties in the war were far greater than was at
first supposed. Not only were the pick of the young men
killed or maimed, but also some twenty million civilians
had died of starvation, disease, or enemy action in Russia
itself and in the slave camps of Hitler's Europe. Millions
more were weakened by undernourishment and overstrain,
many to die prematurely. There were twenty-five million
homeless. Further, as it has now been established beyond
any doubt, the moral health of the Soviet Union was
heavily undermined by the employment of forced labour
on a monstrous scale. And, on top of all this, returned soldiers and civilians, who had seen the West with their own

eyes, were beginning to spread disaffection: even though their impressions of Western life were not so unreservedly favourable as the more complacent among us would like to believe, their influence was considerable. But there will be time to go into these matters when we consider the internal state of the Soviet Union today.

As for the conclusions drawn from my impressions, these were sometimes at fault: I did not then appreciate, for example, the radical nature of the return to Russian nationalism. Also, part of the picture was obscured. It was perfectly clear at that time that the profound Russian impulse to turn away from the West and all its lures was running very strongly; but before many months it was to be demonstrated that I had underestimated the counter-pull, the strength of the expansionist impulse as opposed to the impulse of withdrawal, and the conflict between these two, which is the contemporary expression of the eternal conflict between the Muscovite and Petrine traditions.

Reflections of this kind may still seem meaningless to those who share the common assumption of our time that even during the war Stalin was busily engaged in preparing for the revival of the Comintern and a full-scale Communist onslaught on the outer world. Since this clearly predicated an open return to the Leninist and Trotskyite ideas which had, to put it mildly, been in abeyance since the introduction of "Socialism in One Country," the inference here is that Stalin had never for one moment abandoned the idea of a Moscow-led world revolution, and that therefore all his actions, including the most outrageous deviations from the Marxist line, had in fact been directed firmly, if sometimes obliquely, towards this supreme consummation. The conception of Stalin as a god among men (for nobody less than Jupiter has ever before seen as far

as Stalin is credited with seeing) arose easily, and perhaps
inevitably, from a partial reading of the Bolshevik scriptures and a somewhat doctrinaire consideration of the
course of Soviet action since the war. It was crystallized
out by certain eminent Russia experts in the State Department of the United States, who knew a great deal about
Leninism but rather less about human nature, seized upon
with rapture by politicians and diplomats, who knew nothing about either but were delighted to find a theory into
which current events could be fitted, if on somewhat Pro-
crustean lines, and has now been popularized sufficiently
to penetrate the minds of an American president and a
British prime minister. The cause of all the trouble is the
superficial resurrection of Leninism, which has already
been discussed.

In fact, all the evidence we have points to the conclusion
that, far from having a considered plan of attack, Stalin,
from Teheran onwards, has been improvising in a hand-
to-mouth manner reminiscent of the British Foreign
Office. Until the late summer of 1947 there was no sign
of any plan at all. Mr. Deutscher has dealt very well with
this matter in his biography of Stalin, from which I have
already quoted:

> The question must be asked whether Stalin, while he
> was bargaining for his zone of influence, already con-
> templated putting it under exclusive Communist con-
> trol. Had the scheme of revolution been in his mind at
> the time of Teheran or Yalta? Had it finally taken shape
> at the time of Potsdam? His detractors as well as his
> apologists concur on this point, for both want us to see
> an extremely shrewd and far-sighted design behind his
> actions. Yet Stalin's actions show many strange and strik-
> ing contradictions which do not indicate that he had

any revolutionary master-plan. They suggest, on the contrary, that he had none. Here are a few of the most glaring contradictions. If Stalin consistently prepared to install a Communist government in Warsaw, why did he so stubbornly refuse to make any concessions to the Poles over their eastern frontier? Would it not have been all the same to him whether, say, Lvov, that Polish-Ukrainian city, was ruled from Communist Kiev or from Communist Warsaw? Yet such a concession would have enormously strengthened the hands of the Polish Left. Similarly, if he had beforehand planned revolution for Eastern Germany, why did he detach from Germany and incorporate in Poland *all* the German provinces east of the Neisse and the Oder, of the acquisition of which even the Poles themselves had not dreamt? Why did he insist on the expulsion of the whole German population from these lands, an act that could not but further embitter the German people not only against the Poles but also against Russia and communism. His claim for reparations to be paid by Germany, Austria, Hungary, Rumania, Bulgaria, and Finland, under-standable as it was in view of the devastation of the Ukraine and other Soviet lands, could not but have the same damaging effect on the Communist cause in those countries. This was even truer of Stalin's demand for the liquidation of the bulk of German industry. Already at Teheran, if not earlier, he had given notice that he would raise that demand; at Yalta he proposed that 80 per cent of German industry should be dismantled within two years after the cease fire; and he did not abate that demand at Potsdam. He could not have been unaware that his scheme, as chimerical as ruthless, if it had been carried out, would have entailed the dispersal of the German working class, the main, if not the only, social force to which communism could have appealed and whose support it might have enlisted. Not a single one of these policies can by any stretch of imagination be described as a steppingstone towards revolution. On the contrary, in every one of those moves, Stalin himself was laboriously erecting formidable barriers to revolution. This alone seems to warrant the conclusion that even at the close of the war his intentions were still extremely self-contradictory, to say the least.

I would go even further than Mr. Deutscher and suggest that it is as clear as daylight that in 1945 Russia was above all concerned with scotching the revival of a revanchist Germany, above all by gathering under her influence *as a power* her own border states. The Polish arrangement was intended to serve three separate purposes: to secure for the Soviet Union, as a power, territories which she considered hers (the annexation of Polish Ukraine); to weaken Germany by transferring to Poland the industrial area of Silesia; and to grapple Poland closely to the Soviet Union by making the Poles absolutely dependent on it for protection against German irredentist demands.

What, it seems to me, had happened, looking back, is that until the spring of 1947 Stalin had been thinking more or less consistently in terms of military power. His victorious armies had brought him deep into Europe and he had the chance of a century to establish Russia's influence in those areas where, in the past, it had been steadfastly denied. There was to be no Congress of Berlin to follow this San Stefano, robbing the Russians of the advantage so dearly bought. And, indeed, faced with Messrs. Attlee and Truman, Messrs. Bevin and Byrnes, in place of Disraeli and Salisbury, to say nothing of Bismarck, there must have seemed to Stalin no particular reason why there should be. Instead, there was to be set up a continuous belt of friendly states, isolated from the unsettling influence of Western diplomacy and capital, running from the Baltic to the Adriatic, and including the greater part of the Danube basin. German power was to be kept down. The idea of the "People's Democracy" was a genuine idea, and to Stalin himself not a new one. There is nothing at all to suggest that in 1945 Stalin saw the formal sovietization of Poland, Czechoslovakia, Hungary, and the rest as a goal to be worked for in a hurry. So long as these countries listened to him and not to America and Britain he was content to let them work out their own Socialist destinies. It should be remembered in this context that to Stalin and all his agents some form of totalitarian socialism or state capitalism was the corollary of friendliness in a neighbouring state. In other words, it is improbable that Stalin, in those early days, was any more conscious of interfering with the internal order of, say, Rumania, than the British government and concessionaires had been conscious of interfering with it in their happier days.

That was in the beginning: friendly governments had to be established under the protecting lee of the Red Army while that army was still available. But the Soviet idea of gentle pressure is not the Anglo-Saxon idea. And Anglo-Saxon objections to the production of the whole Bolshevik bag of tricks—single-list elections, police terror, and the rest—all of them as natural and unremarkable to the Politburo as kissing babies to a British member of Parliament or being photographed in lunatic occupations to an American senator—called forth protests from the West and stiffened its attitude in a way which confirmed Stalin in his deep suspicion that Britain and America, and particularly Britain in this context, had no intention at all of abandoning their own commercial interests in East Europe. At the same time the Communist Parties of East Europe were having a great deal of trouble in establishing themselves in a completely unassailable position. Not only that, but some of the Communist leaders were developing independent ideas of their own. We know now, for example, that the Yugoslav Communists were irritating Stalin as early as 1945. Czechoslovakia was not Communist at all, and although it was known in Moscow that Beneš had decided that the future of his country lay in close co-operation with the Russians, there were too many anti-Soviet influences at work in Prague and Bratislava for Stalin, with his obsession with total security, to feel entirely comfortable.

The general world situation was also deteriorating *vis-à-vis* the Soviet Union. Largely as a result of her conduct in the satellites and Germany, the West was being forced into an uncompromising mood. Its firm refusal, first at the London Conference in 1946, finally at the Moscow Conference in 1947, to entertain the Soviet claims for ten billion dollars' worth of German reparations was, more than any other single act, taken by Stalin as a sign that Britain, America, and France were more interested in developing the Ruhr to support a strong Germany than in making Germany pay for the reconstruction of the Soviet Union: the conclusion drawn from this was that the West wished to hinder Soviet reconstruction, a conclusion which the Politburo would leap to all too easily, and which was all too often supported not only by the utterances of irresponsible individuals but also by certain actions by responsible statesmen, such as the insanely abrupt ending of Lend-Lease in 1945. Stalin had repeatedly, from 1944 onwards, welcomed the idea of an American loan or extensive American credits, an idea which was dangled under his nose and then withdrawn. (Mr. Albert Z. Carr, in his book

Truman, Stalin and Peace, has revealing passages on this subject, containing documented information which is not widely known.) His suspicions of Western intentions were active throughout the war and positively inflamed by the long postponement of the so-called Second Front in Europe, the peculiar difficulties of which he never began to grasp. He believed that no matter what assurances the leaders of the West, and especially Roosevelt, might give, hostile pressure would soon make nonsense of them. He saw Mr. Churchill's passion for a Balkan front as a direct barrier to the spread of legitimate Soviet influence. He saw the continued interest of the British in Bulgaria and Rumania, after Mr. Churchill had agreed that these countries should be considered as part of the Soviet zone of influence, as a deliberate double-cross. He saw the reluctance of the richest and most powerful country in the world to assist with the rehabilitation of Russia's ruined economy as an omen of the most sinister kind. And so on.

It is customary for apologists for the Kremlin to say that these, among others, were the things which helped to force the Soviet Union into its present aggressive frame of mind. No doubt they did help. No doubt, also, the Anglo-Saxon powers should be blamed for their policies. But the fact remains that the fundamental responsibility for the drift into chaos belongs to the Soviet government. In 1941 Stalin had the chance of a thousand years to make his peace with the West. He threw that chance away. The events of 1944 onwards which, we are told, gave rise to Stalin's hostility towards the West, did nothing of the kind: they were the response, usually stupid and always muddled, to provocations continuously offered by Stalin from the first days of the German invasion. For three years these provocations were deliberately ignored by the British and American governments, who leant over backwards in their eagerness to let bygones be bygones, to erase bitter memories of the past, and to do nothing at all which might offend the exacerbated sensibilities of the great Russian ally. The history of those years was the history of an uninterrupted series of unpublicized concessions, received by Stalin with no word of thanks or recognition—a series which ended only at Yalta with the public betrayal of Poland. The only just criticism of Allied behaviour towards Russia between 1941 and 1944 is not that we conceded too little to Stalin but that we conceded far too much.

The last thing this book is about, however, is the apportioning of blame between East and West for the present situation. It is possible to make out a case of sorts for Stalin, and elsewhere I have made it; but the question of which side is most to blame in detail must be left for future historians. Our immediate purpose is, acknowledging the conflict, to discover what it amounts to now, how dangerous it is, and what sort of enemy we are called upon to face. To fill in the background of the Cold War I have tried to show that the conception of Stalin as a farsighted and deliberate chess player is an erroneous conception. This is far from being an academic issue, since it must affect our whole approach to the problem before us. The main point I am trying to make is that it was not until the failure of the Moscow Conference in 1947 that Stalin came to the final conclusion that he had temporarily shot his bolt as the leader of a great power, imposing his will on Europe and the world by invoking silently the hidden might of Russia and the prestige of the Red Army. He could either withdraw his strength into the immense fastness of the Soviet Union and apply all his energies to developing his own economy, as so many Russian rulers had done before him after their spectacular excursions into

Europe, as he himself had done in 1928; or he could throw
everything into an attempt to disrupt the economy of the
capitalist world; or he could march his great army across
Europe to the Rhine, or beyond, defying America and
Britain to hit back effectively while he absorbed the industry of Germany and developed the revolution among
the millions of far Asia.

It is commonly believed nowadays that he was only de-
terred from this last course by America's possession of the
atomic bomb. Mr. Churchill has expressed this view many
times; and in due course I shall try to show that it is false.
I myself believed in 1947, as the previous chapter indicates, that Russia would retire upon herself behind a
screen of "friendly," quasi-Communist states, while con-
ducting a harassing campaign against capitalist stability
throughout the world through a not too openly organized
fifth column provided by foreign Communist Parties. I
still think this was Stalin's intention as late as the summer
of 1947. He had gained a good deal, and Russia had paid
heavily for it. His gains had been made possible only by
the most rigorous concealment of Russia's internal weakness and need and on the preservation of an appearance of
strength, based on nothing at all but the physical size of
Russia and the very real prestige of the Red Army. These
were his solitary assets; and employing them had inhibited
him from throwing his cards on the table and showing the
depth and extent of his country's distress. The need, as
we have seen, was so great that its relief now called for all
the energies of every able man in Russia.

Then, out of the blue, in the summer of 1947, came Mr.
Marshall's Harvard speech and the prompt acceptance of
his offer, or challenge, by the British foreign minister. Mr.
Bevin called a conference in Paris to discuss ways and

means of seizing the great opportunity provided by the American offer to help the countries of Europe to help themselves. Did Europe include Russia? Yes, said Mr. Marshall, "I mean everything west of Asia." So Mr. Molotov came too, flying in from Moscow with a following of more than eighty experts and advisers. It was the Kremlin's last chance to get help from the West. For a day or two Mr. Molotov marked time in his well-known manner, offering, to produce an illusion of activity, his own idea of the sort of scheme to work out; but all it amounted to was that each separate country should send in a "shopping list" to Washington, which was not at all what Mr. Marshall wanted, or anybody else. Then, suddenly, without any warning, Mr. Molotov announced that he would play no longer. He had had new instructions, and before the day was out he and his whole imposing following were bundled back into the waiting aircraft and on their way to Moscow.

During these few hours Stalin had taken a decision which was in every way the most important decision of his life; and it may well be that the future historian will look back and see in that decision the action which assured the ultimate downfall of the Soviet régime. The emotion of Mr. Molotov when he walked out of the Paris Conference was very great. It could have been due to nothing but a profound mental disturbance. It was so great that he could not contain himself. "If you continue with this scheme," he burst out, "believe me, you will live to regret it!"

This was the formal declaration of the Cold War.

"Do you think we really deserve this?" Mr. Molotov, pale and drawn, had exclaimed just six years before to the German Ambassador in Moscow, while German airmen bombed the frontier villages of White Russia and the Ukraine.

"Do you think we really deserve this?" Mr. Marshall might have echoed, as the Kremlin embarked on its terrible endeavour to bring ruin to the fields and workshops of half the world.

3

Motives and Aims

THE KREMLIN'S FIRST OBJECT was to confine the Marshall Plan to Western Europe. American wealth, at all costs, had to be prevented from flowing into the satellites. The friendly governments had been established, but there was a great deal of feeling against them. By and large it could be said, and this is especially true of Czechoslovakia, that the peoples of Eastern Europe were clustering round Russia not only out of fear of Germany and a healthy respect for Russian military power, but also by virtue of a strong gravitational pull. Western Europe was supine and void, exercising no material attraction. But if American dollars were now to be used to pull the West together, and if, moreover, the Russian satellites were allowed to share in the resultant prosperity, these would inevitably turn away from Russia and towards the West. Then all the laborious work of the past three years, to say nothing of the fruits of Russia's wartime victories, would go for nothing: sooner or later there would once more be capitalist strongholds

in Warsaw, Prague, Sofia, and all the rest. The very eagerness with which the docile People's Governments argued
the case for their participation in the Marshall Plan
showed Moscow where the danger lay. Prague even said
it would join in, and had to be publicly forced by Stalin
to back out publicly. It was not at all a healthy situation.

Furthermore, even though Stalin could quite easily for-
bid his satellites, or friendly neighbours, to have anything
to do with Western Europe, there would be a very strong
feeling of resentment and bitterness among their populations, and probably their leaders too, at being forced to
pass by this shining opportunity to solve so many weary
problems. And if the Marshall Plan were really to succeed
in its limited field, raising Western Europe out of material
ruin and moral bankruptcy into renewed confidence and
prosperity, then the resentment of the East would know no
bounds, and the new gravitational pull towards the Atlantic would sooner or later prove too strong for the bonds
which then tied the satellites to Russia—bonds which to us
looked like the heaviest of chains but which by the Kremlin's standards of security were hardly more than threads
of gossamer.

The possible place of the Soviet Union as such in the
scheme for Marshall Aid was almost certainly a secondary
consideration. Had she been alone in the world she might
have come in, if only for a limited period, and trusted to
her own wits to obtain the machinery she wanted without
at the same time opening her frontiers to a demoralizing
flow of cheap American consumer goods. Or she might not
have done. But the critical issue was undoubtedly the position of the satellites.

At about this time in Moscow there was raging one of
those furious and esoteric controversies in the higher party
organs which represent the means by which the Politburo

seeks to make its ideological attitude clear to the party intelligentsia. The quarrel this time was between N. A. Voznessensky, himself a member of the Politburo (one of the youngest and most brilliant), as well as the head of the State Planning Commission, and the eminent Professor Varga, an economist of Hungarian birth and Soviet adoption, a protégé of Stalin's, and the recognized authority on capitalist economics. Varga had recorded it as his opinion that the impact of the war on the capitalist economy had caused so mighty a development in the direction of state capitalism and away from unbridled private enterprise that the amended capitalist system might be expected to gain from this a new lease of life, which would postpone the final slump and collapse of that system by a number of years. This was the thesis most vigorously attacked by Voznessensky in the Communist Party monthly, *Bolshevik*. The battle raged (for Varga stuck to his guns) all through 1948, until Varga finally recanted. But by that time, Zhdanov, Voznessensky's chief protector, was dead, and Voznessensky himself had been dismissed from all his posts. The true ins and outs of this affair are impossible to reconstruct. But it is perfectly clear that there was in 1947 a furious discussion going on in the highest government circles as to whether the American postwar slump could be relied upon or not. And it can scarcely be doubted that this debate played a great part in the final decision, terrible and evil, yet in its perverted way also heroic, to cut off the Soviet Union and all the peoples in her sphere of influence finally and irrevocably from all help from the West and to strive with might and main to prevent the West from recovering its prosperity. This prosperity would be so much greater than anything Russia could offer for decades to come that it would soon exert a magnetic attraction on the outposts of the new Soviet

Empire, thus putting an end to the Kremlin's grand system of security.

It is probable, too, that in the Marshall offer those Soviet economists and theoreticians who believed in the imminence of an American slump, which would bring down in ruin all those countries entangled in the American economy, saw the strongest possible confirmation of their views. For they would see in this plan not a generous gesture: there are no such things as generous gestures in international affairs if you are a Russian or a Marxist. Nor would they see in it a response to the Soviet menace: they were unaware of the Soviet menace (it cannot, indeed, be emphasized too much that Soviet actions in East Europe which looked to us like calculated aggression at that time seemed the most natural and unremarkable behaviour in the world to the Russians themselves—just as the behaviour of British oil firms in the Middle East seems natural and unremarkable to Englishmen; and just as, for example, the employment of the Most-Favoured-Nation Clause to undermine the British Empire seems the most natural and unremarkable thing to Americans—so natural and unremarkable, in fact, that most of them are unaware of it). Seeing neither a generous gesture nor the response to Soviet aggression, the Russian observer would see in it only the long-awaited sign: Mr. Marshall was out to save the American businessmen from disaster by blackmailing Europe into providing them with new markets, thus, at Europe's expense, staving off catastrophe a little longer.

At any rate, the war was on. In November 1947 the Cominform was inaugurated at Warsaw by Messrs. Zhdanov and Malenkov. The original idea of the People's Democracies, a *sui generis* system for the friendly bastions of Soviet security, was no longer enough. The satellites could no longer be left independent. Yugoslavia was already giving serious signs of independent thinking and, in spite of repeated rebuffs from the West, which had written Prague off too soon, the Czechs were very far from being as secure as Moscow liked. We know now that Stalin was preparing for a showdown with Marshal Tito for some time before the world was aware of it. He was to be the awful example of what happened to Russia's protégés if they questioned their master's ways. And it is quite clear that the decision to do away with the last relics of Czech independence in June of that year was tied in with the coming demonstration against the Yugoslavs.

As far as the outside world was concerned the plan was quite simply to frustrate the European Recovery Programme and any kind of Western Union, seen as an anti-Russian coalition including Western Germany. This was to be achieved by exploiting not only the differences between the Western peoples and their governments and the differences between the various Western governments themselves, but also by stirring up and canalizing unrest in the backward and colonial areas of the world with the aim of destroying the main props of the capitalist economy. At the same time, the Eastern European satellite states were to be more closely integrated into the Soviet economy. In case there is any doubt at all about this, we have not only the generalized authority of Lenin himself, already cited earlier in this book, but also, in up-to-date form, the plan of campaign officially outlined by L. P. Beria, the late chief policeman of Russia, and now one of the three men ruling the Soviet Union in Stalin's name. In an article written for *Pravda* on Stalin's seventieth birthday in December 1949, he said:

Stalin has laid down a programme of action for Communists. They must:

1. Exploit all differences and contradictions in the bourgeois camp.

2. Take concrete action to unite the working classes of the economically advanced countries with the liberation movement in the colonies and dependent nations.

3. Complete the struggle for unity of the trade-union movement.

4. Take active measures to bring together the proletariat and the small peasants.

5. Support Soviet rule and disrupt the interventionist machinations of imperialism against the Soviet Union, bearing in mind that the Soviet Union is the base of the revolutionary movement in all countries.

In actual practice these instructions work out in this way:

1. Set all countries in the world against America and, where possible, against each other as well; develop and exploit all differences between classes, seizing every legitimate grievance to foster strikes, and, where legitimate ones do not exist, manufacture imaginary ones.

2. Strive to make the workingmen of Europe take sides against their governments in favour of Indonesian, Malayan, Korean, and African nationalism. Make them express their solidarity by refusing to load or manufacture arms to be used against these peoples.

3. Set yourselves the task of dominating the Western trade unions by skilful infiltration, where necessary under cover.

4. Do not ignore the revolutionary potential of the illiterate peasants, however much you may despise them, above all in places like the more backward areas of Italy.

5. Back the Soviet government against your own in every detail and particular. The first loyalty of every Communist is to the Soviet Union. Use every means in your power to discredit the efforts of your governments to unite against the Soviet Union, and above all play on popular bewilderment and infirmity of purpose by identifying the Soviet Union with the cause of peace.

And so on.

Mr. Beria's five paragraphs, in a word, provide an admirable official outline of the plan of campaign for the Cold War. For the rest, the answers will be provided by the judicious exercise of Soviet military might. Good Communists need not bother their heads about that, except on each and every occasion to deny it. Nor need they be told that their own part in the Cold War is not directed towards the greater glory of Marxism, which Stalin is no longer interested in for its own sake, but only for the survival and greater glory of the Soviet Union as the monstrous re-embodiment of the Tsarist Empire of Great Russia.

4

Russia and Germany

THE MORE WE LOOK at the Kremlin with that detachment so desirable in contemplating alien manifestations of life, the more untenable appears to be the notion that in every Soviet move we may see the slow, deliberate unfolding of a master plan of extreme complexity and infinite far-sightedness. Nothing brings this home more strongly than a consideration of Stalin's policy towards Germany, unless, possibly, the affair of Marshal Tito, which we examine in the next chapter. The German policy is worth looking at in some detail because it is of supreme importance in Stalin's eyes, because it covers not only the period of the Cold War to date, but also, in one sweep, the whole course of Soviet thinking since Yalta, and because we can start from a known and irrefutable fact, namely, that Stalin is afraid of Germany.

In considering his German policy we have to start from that one fact which, in all the excitement about the Kremlin's rearming of Germany, is apt to be overlooked. Stalin has good reason to be afraid. Germany, a people of 70 millions, all but finished off the Soviet Union, a people of 200 millions, while fighting half the world besides. In the process of being beaten, Germany laid waste European Russia, caused the death of some 10 million Russian soldiers and some 20 million civilians, and reduced Soviet industrial production by half. If she was left to herself, or given the assistance of the Western Allies, there was nothing to stop Germany, after a pause for recuperation, from repeating her performance of 1941.

Thus it became a cardinal point in Stalin's policy to see that Germany was not left to herself and was not driven into the arms of an inimically disposed Western Alliance. How did he set about attaining these ends?

At the end of the war, as a result of agreements reached earlier, Russia found herself occupying the Eastern zone of a Germany divided among the four wartime Allies, each of whom also had a share in Berlin; the declared aim was to establish a quadripartite military government of the whole country, treated as a single economic unit. Russia's most intelligent course would have been to get on to the best possible terms with America, France, and Britain and devise with them a common policy for keeping Germany demilitarized and disarmed. But she was inhibited from this for doctrinal reasons. Temporary cooperation with the bourgeois powers was feasible; but the scotching of the German menace forever called for permanent cooperation, and this, according to the Bolshevik canon, was out of the question.

Thus Russia's only hope, as the Kremlin saw it, was to manage Germany herself and work for the transformation of the whole of Germany into a Russian satellite. This consummation would not only remove the menace of Germany, but would also provide Russia with an enormous increase of strength in face of the Anglo-Saxon powers and France. She did, indeed, follow this course, but with insufficient single-mindedness and boldness until it was too late; and by then she had ruined her chances, such as they were, by pursuing incidental aims which conflicted with the main purpose.

By absorbing the Polish Ukraine up to the Curzon Line and allowing the Poles to take a compensating slice of Germany up to the Oder-Neisse Line, the Kremlin allowed two short-term aims to cut across its one supreme aim, as we have already seen. Furthermore, the expulsion of the German inhabitants of the Polish "Recovered Territories," and of the Sudetenland too, made it inevitable that both the Czechs and the Poles would fear a German military revival more than anything else in the world and look to Russia for support in face of it—support which they would have to pay for by total surrender to Russian demands. This is the kind of plan which looks beautiful on the desk of the Moscow foreign office, a cunning plan, a plan as calculated as a game of chess. But chess is a game played on a fixed board of sixty-four squares: international politics are played on a fluid basis. By securing the Western Ukraine for herself and ensuring Polish and Czech subservience out of fear of Germany, Russia made it that much more difficult for herself ever to win control of Germany. And although she contrived to keep something in hand for future developments—namely, that large part of East Prussia which she took for herself and could always, if occasion arose, make over to Poland in exchange for a compromise adjustment of the Oder-Neisse Line in favour of Germany (a docile Germany, of course)—the harm she had done to her chances in Germany by turning loose a horde of refugees from the East could not easily be wiped out.

It is not as though the Germans were in a mood to like the Russians. All Germany, right up to the Elbe, had seen first the Russian soldiery, then the Russian police, both at their worst in the semblance of a barbarian horde; and it is to be doubted whether the Kremlin has given proper weight to this fact. On top of that, immediately after victory, came the organized looting of the Eastern zone. So that the situation between Russia and Germany, when the Foreign Ministers' Treaty discussions were breaking down in London in 1946 and in Moscow in 1947, was about as bad as it could be.

There was no question at all but that Russia desperately and urgently needed, and deserved, reparations on the largest possible scale. This need had driven her to loot the Eastern zone, isolating it from the German economy as a whole, and withholding promised deliveries to the Western zones. Somewhere in Stalin's mind, no doubt, was the vague calculation that by intensifying famine and economic collapse in the West he was not only fanning the flames of revolution there but also putting further burdens on the British and American taxpayers, which could help to divide those two powers. In fact, the first thing that happened was that the Western zones retaliated by withholding deliveries to the Eastern zone, thereby crippling it still further. At the same time, the Western foreign ministers were driven to resist with flat negatives all claims for reparations from current production and all claims for Russian participation in control of the Ruhr, until such time as Russia threw open the Eastern zone to the quadripartite control of all Germany as a single economic unit. By sealing off the Eastern zone for the sake of immediate loot, Russia had, in a word, killed the goose that laid the golden egg.

By that time—certainly by early 1947—the Kremlin must

have given up all hope of a spontaneous revolution in Russia's favour. The only hope for Russian control of all Germany now lay in the setting up of a centralized German government which could be lured or intimidated into the Russian camp on lines akin to the manœuvres then being prepared for the bloodless conquest of Czechoslovakia—the classic example of a revolution from above. Because of this, Mr. Molotov resisted all attempts by the Western Allies to establish a federal constitution, which would have denied the East German Communists the chance to gain control of all Germany through a centralized machine directed from Moscow. The only conceivable hope the Kremlin had of getting a central government was by relaxing its grip on the Eastern zone. This, for one reason and another, it would not, or could not, do. And so the gulf remained, and the Western powers reacted first by merging their zones, then by forcing through the currency reform which put an end to the Kremlin's hopes of breeding chaos from chaos in the West, then by preparing the formal statute setting up a West German government.

The Kremlin's plans had gone very much awry. Stalin had been forced to abandon the idea of spontaneous revolution; he had manœuvred himself into a position in East Germany which completely ruled out any hope of a central German government capable of carrying out the revolution from above; he had cut himself off from reparations which he still desperately needed; and now he was faced with a united Western Germany, containing two-thirds of the German population, the great bulk of Germany's heavy industry, and eight million refugees from the East who, far from helping to create a revolutionary situation, lived only for the day when they could return to their homes. What Stalin had in exchange, apart from his precious Lvov and a chunk of the Ukraine, was a good deal of loot, a Poland and a Czechoslovakia clinging to him for fear of Germany, and an endless source of mischief. He also had one trump card: the impossible position of the Western Allies in Berlin. He decided to play this card, with the immediate object of stopping the setting up of a West German government before it was too late, and with the general object of forcing the Western foreign ministers into suing for further talks. In both objects he failed, and after the amazing (and to the Kremlin quite shattering) success of the Air Lift, it found itself as before—or rather, with the situation worsened by a quasi-diplomatic defeat of the first magnitude.

It was time, one would have said, for the Kremlin to think again; and there are signs that a great deal of fairly radical thinking was done about this time. What sustained it in its original determination was the profound conviction that the United States was riding for a fall and, by running into economic disaster, would bring about the collapse of Marshallized Western Europe. Thus, while doing everything in its power to hinder European recovery and undermine Anglo-Saxon stability in Asia, the Kremlin concentrated on integrating Eastern Germany into the satellite economic bloc, lulling the fears of the Poles and the Czechs, and building up in East Germany a puppet government based on an armed force which could take over and subdue the whole country at the first sign of the collapse of Western power. It is fairly clear that up to the spring of 1950 the Kremlin believed, owing to its extremely faulty intelligence, that the mood of the West Germans was far more favourable to Russia than it was. There is no doubt at all that the "capture" of Berlin by East German forces was planned for the Whitsun of 1950; and there is no doubt at all that this plan was abandoned. Meanwhile, however, by its efforts all over the world to divide the Western Allies and accelerate their economic collapse, above all by frightening Western Europe into a state of fatalistic submission in face of Soviet might, the Kremlin had also succeeded in stimulating America into a state of angry belligerence. Also, by forming and arming the East German *Bereitschaften*, it had given the West a pretext for rearming Western Germany. The Korean affair, which threw a lurid light on the potentialities of Russian-sponsored nationalist armies, brought us where we are today.

Now, as it seems to me, the Kremlin and its puppet governments in Poland and Czechoslovakia are contemplating the rearmament of Western Germany with an extremity of fear which we find it hard to imagine. And this brings us back to the beginning—to the hard fact of the Kremlin's justifiable fear of Germany. In spite of all its propaganda, the Kremlin probably does not fear imminent American aggression. But looking at the eight million refugees from the East, who will form the main element in any West German army, it is convinced that, even if they so desire, the Atlantic powers will be unable to restrain the quite publicly announced determination of these expatriates to go home.

This is not a very impressive record. Not to put too fine a point on it, it is a classic example of Russian ineptitude. In face of it, it is surely impossible to sustain the illusion that the Russians are extremely gifted diplomats—an illusion which seems to rest on a very insecure foundation. It takes more than a poker face, a gift for telling lies, and a propensity for elaborate and unscrupulous calculation to succeed in diplomacy. More than any of these, it takes intelligence and common sense and a certain freedom of approach to unexplored ground. We have seen enough of the Russians in these pages to know that these are precisely the last qualities to be expected in a Soviet diplomat; and the Kremlin's handling of the German problem, it seems to me, confirms in practice what we have already observed in theory. One of Stalin's main preoccupations from 1944 onwards has been to hamstring German militarism and lay the German menace once and for all; yet his diplomacy has succeeded in reviving that menace, as he sees it, in a shorter time than anyone would have thought possible. Perhaps it has been Mr. Molotov's diplomacy, not Stalin's; but if Stalin is not responsible for Mr. Molotov, I do not know who is.

It is a record of failure of the most ignominious kind. And whether the reader inclines to Mr. Deutscher's belief that Stalin has been more or less blindly groping forward from crisis to crisis or to my own belief that he has been trying to do too many things, some of them contradictory, at one and the same time, does not matter. The point at issue is that, for whatever reasons, neither Stalin nor his advisers can qualify as the architects of deep-laid, subtle, and farsighted schemes, to say nothing of an elaborate plot, winding its way through decades of upheaval, to subdue the whole world. They may, indeed, conspire, but, as I remarked much earlier, the will is not the same as the deed. And it should be clear by now that the so-called grand design of Moscow, when examined in the cold light of day, is turning out to be little more than the outcome of contradictory pressures, external and domestic, on a group of men who cannot get it out of their heads that they are immune to such pressures, and thus make confusion worse.

5

Tito and the Satellites

IT IS POSSIBLE TO ARGUE that some of the ineptitudes, muddles, and desperate improvisations attributed to Stalin in previous chapters have not been ineptitudes, muddles, and desperate improvisations at all, but only appear so because the full course of the grand design has not been run. Indeed, it is possible to argue almost anything, including the thesis that by coldly betraying Mao Tse-tung and supporting Chiang Kai-shek (as Stalin did over a great many years) the Kremlin was consciously doing the Chinese Communists a good turn—though it is to be hoped that these themselves know better! But there is one thing that cannot be argued (although people hypnotized by Soviet power tried very hard to do so for a time), namely, that Stalin knew what he was doing when he pronounced anathema on Marshal Tito.

Thus the first and most important thing about the Tito affair is precisely that it does demonstrate conclusively, once and for all, that the Kremlin can and does make mistakes, and that to imagine that it is infallible and invulnerable is to play straight into the hands of the Communists, who devote their miserable lives to trying to make it seem so. The members of the Moscow Politburo are, as human beings, fallible; while in so far as they are still Leninists, their whole philosophy is rooted in error—or so those of us who are not Leninists must believe. And yet we attribute to these preposterous representatives of a backward country, running a system based on false premises, a subtlety and prescience unexampled in the history of the world. Perhaps those who have not followed me so far will meditate on the Tito blunder and ask themselves whether the men who can perpetrate one howler on this massive scale may not, after all, have perpetrated others. It might also be a good thing to ask whether their very insistence on the supreme importance of theory and planning does not give them away. For the only people who have to take theory seriously are those without an instinctive sense of reality; and the only people who have to take planning seriously are those without an instinctive sense of order.

If our first debt of gratitude to Tito—whether we approve of him or not—is for his simple exposure of the Kremlin at a loss, the second is for his daring to call Stalin's bluff. This is an aspect of the Tito affair which has not received the attention it deserves, perhaps because we shrink from its implications. But the fact remains that the head of this small, vulnerable, almost completely encircled state, a state, moreover, deficient in national unity, has dared to stand up to the Soviet Union more radically and steadfastly than the greatest powers in the world. Whether inspired by faith or by superior intelligence as to the real state of affairs inside the Soviet Union and the satellite ring, or by the sort of attitude which lies behind

this book, Tito has said to Stalin in effect, "I do not believe in your threats and I am ready to stake all I have
on calling your bluff." For about three years he has main-
tained that position in face of the united execrations of
his Cominform neighbours and the darkest threats of
violence. For a great part of that time he has sustained an
economic blockade imposed at the very moment when the
Yugoslav economy is at its most vulnerable. If this is not
a lesson to the rest of us—a lesson which makes its point
whether Tito is ultimately done away with or not—then I
don't know what is.

A third service performed involuntarily by Marshal Tito
is his forcing of the Kremlin's hand. He has compelled
Stalin to show the true logic of his attitude towards the
satellites sooner and more precipitately than he would
otherwise, I think, have done. He may even, as I believe,
have brought about an actual change of policy. For by
defying Moscow so steadfastly he has compelled Moscow to
admit in effect that its real interests lie not in the spread
of the Communist ideology as such but, and for whatever
purpose, in Russian imperialism. Furthermore, having
once had to throw off its ideological camouflage, the Moscow Politburo has given up all pretence behind the Iron
Curtain everywhere that its interest is anything but dominion by force. This demonstration has opened the eyes
of many simple souls who were far from being fellow
travellers, as well as heavily disillusioning not only fellow
travellers but some hitherto loyal party members.

Finally, we must not overlook the effect of Tito's revolt
on the Kremlin itself. The psychological shock was certainly profound. But, more than this, it was an unsettling
experience. We have already seen that Stalin and his
friends are not by any means so completely obsessed with
their own readings of Marxist-Leninism as they pretend.

They are nevertheless, as I have said, still very much the prisoners of the Marxist attitude, and they are accustomed to justifying all their own actions and condemning all the actions of others in quasi-Marxist terms. But in the Tito affair, for the first time in many years, they are up against a major event which cannot be explained away, by any stretch of the imagination, in even pseudo-quasi-Marxist terms. It is easy enough to pretend that Messrs. Attlee and Morrison are in the pay of Wall Street or that the British coal magnates themselves invented nationalization as a convenient way of passing on their losses to the nation (indeed, one sometimes, shivering, wonders). But to explain exactly what has happened in Yugoslavia in terms which would convince a child calls for an appreciation of reality, of the way the world works—the world of human beings behaving like human beings—which is not fostered by a close study of *Problems of Leninism*. The actual explanation offered is that Tito is a spy and always was one; but it took the Kremlin some time to commit itself to that assertion, and too many Communists know it to be a lie.

In these aspects, as well as in others not mentioned, the Tito affair has an importance which has not even yet, I think, been widely enough realized. It falls very nicely into line with the general thesis of this book—which, it may already be suspected, is that Stalin and his friends are not, to put it vulgarly, all they are cracked up to be, and that Soviet Russia, even if she has not feet of clay (plaster of Paris, perhaps?), has, to put it politely, her fair share of those internal contradictions in which Karl Marx, with the light of battle in his eyes, saw the downfall of organized societies. Even those who set themselves most determinedly against the present Yugoslav régime, who see in Tito, his quarrel with Stalin notwithstanding, simply a pocket replica of Stalin, should be glad that he is what he has proved to be. Indeed, the very worst that can be said against Tito the independent is that he can bring no more woe to the people of Yugoslavia than can Tito the most ardent and impatient of Stalin's disciples.

The first thing we have to ask, if we wish to derive any benefit from this affair, is why Russia let it happen—or rather why, having blundered into letting it happen, she has allowed Tito to survive for three years.

Russia let it happen, obviously, because she did not know any better; it simply never occurred to her that, especially after the lesson of Finland, a weak country would defy her. The immediate and obvious answer to the question why has she allowed Tito to survive so long is surely that she could do nothing else.

Certainly the Kremlin has tried to pull Tito down. It has uttered threats of a kind probably never before heard in time of technical peace between nations. It has demonstrated with troops on Yugoslavia's frontiers, and fomented incidents. It has appealed to anti-Tito elements inside Yugoslavia to rise against the government and turn it out. It has declared that it is the solemn duty of Communists everywhere to fight against Tito. And, above all, it has imposed an economic blockade designed to ruin the Yugoslav economy—a blockade, moreover, which is by no means painless for the other satellites, especially Czechoslovakia and Poland, who have both suffered very heavily from their interrupted trade with Yugoslavia. But with all this, three years have passed. Tito still stands, and the Kremlin has not yet tried the most effective way of removing him— or driving him from Belgrade—namely, war—war open or war disguised in the Spanish manner.

Since, as we have seen, the Kremlin has no moral scruples about war whatsoever, the elementary conclusion is that so far the Kremlin has felt that it cannot safely go to war with Tito. It may also have believed—indeed, it should so believe, if all it has said about the failure of E.R.P. and the imminence of the American slump is still taken seriously in Moscow—that the economic blockade, laced with a lively and persistent war of nerves, will sooner or later make Tito's position untenable. But if the Soviet Union is really as fit for war as so many people have been making out, we should surely have expected some sort of military intervention long ago. The most familiar argument for the Kremlin's warlike intentions is the "face" argument. Surely, having stuck her neck out so far, Russia must go through with it if only to save her own face. That is how the argument runs, but it holds a fallacy. The Russians have never been interested in face, but only in force. What they hold is held not by prestige but by policemen. It is only in the initial stages of a new and predatory move that the Russians rely on the prestige of their might to paralyse their victims in advance. When it comes to running a secured imperium they have never relied on face, and they know it. They have never cared about that sort of thing at all. If the tsars had really cared for face they would never have given way at the Congress of Berlin. If Stalin had cared for face he would never have dared commit his innumerable treacheries on the foreign Communist Parties. The most that can be said is that if the Kremlin was bent on intimidating an adjoining small state into subjection it might think twice about showing weakness in face of Tito. But for the time being there are no more suitably placed small states to be intimidated; and there is also every reason to suppose that the Kremlin has advanced as far into Europe as it proposes or desires for some time to come. If this is so, the argument that Russia cannot afford to drop Tito like a hot potato and go back on her word means nothing. The Bolsheviks have done little else in their thirty years of power but drop things like hot potatoes and go back on their word. They cared little for the face they lost over the Molotov-Ribbentrop Pact or over the betrayal of the German Communists. By their particular mode of calculating (which is nevertheless, in the long run, a faulty mode) these betrayals cost them nothing. As for the face argument, this is an example of the sort of confusion that can arise by thinking of the Russians as Orientals (I take it on trust that the true Oriental is in fact a believer in face). They are not Orientals; they are Russians. And it says something for their wholly contemptuous attitude towards such refinements of honour that nobody at all, not even America and the British Empire with all their might, has yet drawn the obvious conclusion from Russian weakness in face of Tito. Both these two mighty powers let Tito face the dragon, while they themselves shiver with fright in the shadows and babble about the bombing of New York. . . .

But if this particular argument—the argument that the Kremlin *must* crush Tito for reasons of prestige—holds no water, prestige is not the only reason for a possible armed attack on Yugoslavia, and the fact that no such attack has so far been launched does not mean that it never will be. It is only possible to say for certain in this context that the whole training of the Communist Party is against any sort of aggressive war that cannot be finished quickly, and that this is reinforced by the traditional Russian reluctance to storm a strong position if it can be undermined. Add to that the almost certain fact that the Soviet Union is, as I shall soon try to show, in no fit state to risk embroiling herself in a total war, either materially or morally, and the chances against anything like an open attack, either by the Soviet army or by the satellite armies surreptitiously reinforced by the Russians, are pretty heavy.

In this connection, too, we have to ask whether the reconquest of Yugoslavia and the substitution of a Soviet puppet for Tito would really be to the advantage of the Kremlin for some years to come. The opportunity for seizing Greece has gone, and the chief value of Yugoslavia is as a steppingstone to Greece. Furthermore, we may also ask whether Tito the villain, the Trotskyite, and the scapegoat may not (as reckoned in the tortuous calculations of the Moscow Central Committee) be more valuable alive than dead as a cover and a pretext for the new rule of force in the other satellites—a rule which Tito himself precipitated. The extraordinary way in which he has been built up by the Moscow propagandists suggests that this question may not be farfetched. Instead of playing Tito down, and pretending that he does not matter, the Kremlin has done everything in its power to build him up as the archenemy from whom all evils flow—and there are plenty of evils in the satellites to be accounted for. This buildup has gone, of course, hand in hand with the campaign to eliminate from the European consciousness the fact that Tito was ever a Communist; and the "loyal" Yugoslav Communists are thereby, by implication, written down into the same category as the Communists of France or Italy —comrades who will one day be gathered into the arms of the great father but who must for the time being plough a lonely furrow. At the same time the figure of Tito the heretic has become completely obliterated by the figure of Tito the veteran Anglo-American spy. And all this seems to me to suggest very strongly that whatever limited campaigns the Kremlin may pursue, using Bulgaria, for example, as a stalking-horse and Macedonian independence as a rallying point for an internal Yugoslav opposition, its real policy is, as it were, to write off the Yugoslav corner of the map as something which threatens the Cominform, in the way that Wall Street threatens the Cominform, but in which the Cominform has no special and proprietorial interest.

Far more important than what Russia is doing to Yugoslavia, it seems to me, is what she is doing to the remaining satellites, either as a result of Tito's defection or using this defection as a pretext—to such an extent that it is hardly too much to say that if Tito had not occurred it would have been necessary for Stalin to invent him.

For what she has done, with the purges and trials and the virtual transformation of the Cominform organization into a branch of the Soviet Security Police, is quite deliberately to kill the spirit of the Communist Party in Eastern Europe. This is done by behaving towards its most ardent and devoted leaders in exactly the same way as those Communist leaders themselves behaved towards their Socialist colleagues of the Popular Fronts. In other words, the late loyal servants of Moscow, Rajk of Hungary, Kostov of Bulgaria, Gomulka of Poland, have received a large dose of their own precious medicine. For just as they allied themselves with the Socialists, only to kill them off when they had climbed with them into power, so they find themselves being discarded once they have fulfilled their function of establishing the Kremlin's power over their own countries.

This extraordinary process, besides physically removing those Communist leaders who have any taint of independent thought, or who might be suspected of developing such a taint, has broken the hearts of the best and most active elements of the Eastern European Communist Parties, has killed the spirit of communism in Eastern Europe, has thrown overboard that hard core of convinced fanatics which would have proved Russia's most valuable asset if the further spread of communism here and now

were the Politburo's main preoccupation. This, as we have
already seen, is a characteristically Russian, as distinct from
Bolshevik, performance. It throws away goodwill as a sentimental extravagance—as Russia threw away the goodwill of
the West after the late war. It kills the ardent proselytizing
spirit by drowning it in disillusionment—because the
proselytizing spirit has achieved all that was required of
it (the conquest of Eastern Europe in this case) and is no
longer necessary. In so doing, in this immense display of
ruthless cynicism, all that Russia is achieving in exchange
for its missionary supporters is a cowed and acquiescent
rank and file, ready to obey orders and nothing more.

The obvious conclusion from this is that at the present
stage of the world situation the Moscow Politburo has decided that servility and obedience on the part of discour-
aged populations are worth more than active warriors
devoted to the Communist cause. It is impossible to tell
whether the example of Tito so rattled the Politburo, coming when it did in the struggle with the West, that it felt
itself driven to reduce the remaining satellites to a level of
hopelessness from which no insurrection could possibly
spring, or whether the example of Tito is simply being
used as a pretext for accelerating a predetermined policy.
But it is quite clear, I think, that Tito's challenge has had
a great deal to do with the timing of this development and,
in one way and another, forced the Kremlin's hand. And
this is important. It brings us round to our beginning,
which was to dissociate Russia and communism. Russia is
Russia, an unsettling influence in the world, timeless, a
formidable force, but shot through with spectacular weaknesses, and certainly, as Russia, not concerned with the
conquest of the world but only with assuring her own
dominant position. Communism as a revolutionary movement is also formidable, but, unless we believe in its

premises, by no means to be considered as timeless. Russia and communism taken separately can neither of them conquer the world. But Russia and communism taken together form a combination terrible indeed. It has been the extraordinary accident of association between eternal Russia and a genuine movement, however misguided in application, to improve the human lot that has thrown the world into its present confusion, each blurring the true outlines of the other, so that the rest of us have become virtually incapable of seeing them individually for what they are. And the great historical importance of Tito is that he has brought into the open for all to see that divorce between Russia and Marxism which we have already traced in the occasional speeches of Stalin and the patient burrowings of the Soviet historians quietly engaged in working for the glory of Great Russia behind the rolling barrage of Marxist-Leninist propaganda: propaganda which in Russia itself provides the ruling class with a body of hocus-pocus which offers the answer to every question as well as a sense of continuity, and outside Russia harnesses the energies of Communists everywhere to the Kremlin's egocentric purpose.

4. *Cracks in the Kremlin Wall*

1

The Submerged Ten Million

Any appreciation of the state of Russia today must be in the nature of a personal statement. There are not enough documented facts to form a picture, and no single eyewitness has seen enough of the Soviet Union to speak with authority on the whole from his own experience. The approach to the truth about Russia is a slow and laborious progress. Let me give an example. Immediately after the war, in 1946, I wrote a book which was above all an impressionistic survey of Russia as observed during two wartime years, backed by a good deal of reading. The book contained several references to the power of the police and the institution of forced labour, which shocked some enthusiasts. These included an impression of a labour camp, seen from the outside, a close-up description of a gang of prisoners building a new port in the depth of the arctic winter, and some account of the methods of the Security Police and the terrors of midnight arrest and deportation. There was also a short account of a scene at Sizran railway station in the autumn of 1941 where some hundreds of Volga Germans were waiting in closed cattle trucks, sidetracked in the snow, on their long journey to the East— some hundreds of the two hundred thousand who made that same journey. Taken all together, there was enough to show violence, the exercise of arbitrary power, the existence of an extremity of human misery in a land which claimed to be a citadel of light. But that was all; and it was all there could be. At that time I myself believed that the scenes sketched in that book were characteristic of the sort of thing that was going on all over the Soviet Union: everything pointed that way. There were the admissions in the Soviet press before the war (for example, the figure of 250,000 prisoners employed at one time on the digging of the Baltic-White Sea Canal, under Yagoda, then head of the G.P.U.); there were the prewar reports of escaped or released prisoners, occasional and fragmentary; there were the repeated, undemonstrative references to arrests and disappearances in every Russian family; there was the evident belief among the Russian people that the labour camps lay in wait for all who stepped across a certain obscurely drawn line, and the consequent demoralization in high places and low; there were the mysterious disappearances among one's official contacts and the visible embarrassment of their colleagues when the absent ones were mentioned; there were memories of the liquidation of the kulaks and of the great purges of the thirties; above all, there were the tales of Polish prisoners amnestied after the Stalin-Sikorsky Pact of 1941, and the physical appearance of those who still lived as they made their way from the prison camps of the north to the reception centres of General Anders' army at Kuibyshev and Buzuluk; there were stories told by Russians who still dared talk against the régime; there were the admissions of officials and Com-

munists and their supporters, who seemed not to realize
how much they were admitting.

But all that was not enough. It was wartime, and the
Soviet Union was fighting for its bare existence in conditions of extreme hunger and unexampled savagery. In the
harshness of life in Russia at that time, and the courage
and endurance with which the people bore this harshness,
it was impossible to tell whether the gangs of half-starved
scarecrows dressed in rags who shovelled snow from the
airfields, made up the main roads, cut wood in the forests,
were formal prisoners, free citizens temporarily conscripted
for special tasks in an emergency, or self-sacrificing volun-
teers. Again, to set against the horror, there were innumerable examples of Russians returning from forced labour
in good spirits and with no outward rancour. Thus, no
matter how deeply one suspected that Russia had become
a vast prison camp, it was impossible to be certain, to say
nothing of proving it objectively.

Since then things have changed. A mass of new evidence
has accumulated. The scenes described in my book may
now be seen as characteristic, not exceptional. But alas, the
matter does not end there. We are dealing with Russia, not
Western Europe. All that has been proved is, precisely,
that coercion, expressing itself in police rule and slave
labour, is part of the Soviet system, and a large part of it.
A fact has been established; but there still remains the
interpretation of the fact. Briefly, is the Soviet penal system the expression of an evil peculiar to the Stalin régime,
which would vanish were the régime to vanish, leaving a
free and happier Russia? Or should it rather be seen as
in some way analogous to the iniquitous English penal system in the early days of the English industrial revolution—
a system under which men were executed, sent to the
hulks, transported to the Antipodes, for the most trivial of

crimes—a system which was all of a piece with the tolerance of child labour in the mills and of women acting as draught beasts in the mines? And, if so, does forced labour in intolerable conditions appear to the Russians, the mass of the Russians, in anything like the same light as it appears to us? And may not Russia grow out of her present police system, as England grew out of hanging men for stealing sheep such a very short time ago? This is the sort of question that has to be asked and answered in any search for the truth about Russia. It is not enough to prove that the Soviet system is in many ways a system of extreme barbarity. We have to ask why. And we have to ask whether what is barbarous in our eyes seems barbarous to Russians. Upon the answers to these questions depends our whole interpretation of the Soviet fact—and therefore of the real nature of the enemy.

In 1914, under the last of the tsars, there were some thirty thousand Russians serving terms of penal servitude, or *katorga*. This punishment was quite distinct from ordinary imprisonment for criminal or political offences and also from the punishment, confined to rebellious intellectuals, of exile. There were various degrees of exile, as there are today, the commonest and most moderate being a simple prohibition from living in certain main cities or deportation to specific provincial towns. Under the tsars many towns in Siberia, and also in European Russia, were populated almost exclusively by exiles, reporting every so often to the chief of police, but otherwise free to live as best they could, very often on the best of terms with the local governor. This continues under Stalin, and the proportion of the inhabitants of a town like Omsk who are living there against their will is very high indeed. They are not in disgrace; they are merely prevented from moving freely about the country and consorting with their old acquaintances and friends. I myself knew an elderly tsarist general who had been living exiled in Tashkent, or thereabouts, for twenty years in fairly stricken circumstances; but during the war, at the time of Stalingrad, he was flown up to Moscow and consulted by the Kremlin on certain aspects of the fighting over ground he knew very well. Afterwards he was flown back again. Incidentally, it is this strong infusion of independent spirits which makes Siberian society so much livelier than society in the great cities of European Russia.

Under Stalin a new form of exile has grown up. A good engineer, a good doctor, a good plant pathologist will find himself transported for some small political offence to the remote regions of Kamchatka, there to spend his days pursuing his own work, usually better paid and with more privileges than he would ever receive at home, but cut off indefinitely from his wife and family. Since almost every Russian commits some small political offence sooner or later, it is clear that the offence is used only as a pretext for getting a good man where he is wanted.

Finally, there is the system of mass exile, or deportation. During the collectivization millions of so-called kulaks were transported to Siberia and settled on new land. Since at this time the Kremlin was above all interested in developing the virgin agricultural lands of the east and the south, it is impossible to say whether the overruling motive behind these deportations was to get the kulaks away from their familiar ground or to use their opposition to collectivization as a pretext for moving them onto undeveloped ground. These mass deportations have continued, and during the war, and since, they have grown to enormous proportions. As we have seen, the whole of the population of the Volga German Republic was bodily moved under shocking conditions from the area round

Kuibyshev and Saratov to Kazakhstan. This was for security reasons. After the war the Crimean Tartars were removed from the Crimea and the Chechens and the Ingushes from the Caucasus. This was done as a punishment for their disloyalty in the fight with Hitler. Into the empty farms came Russians, White Russians, and Ukrainians, above all the latter. Indeed, it seems to be true to say that something like half the working population of Uzbekistan, Kazakhstan and the Maritime Province in the Soviet Far East is now Ukrainian—the object here being to dilute the population of the Ukraine itself, always, with its separatist dreams, a fortress of resistance to the central Moscow government. The Jews have also been shifted from the western borderlands, and Great Russian settlers have been moved westwards in their place.

Operations of this kind are carried out with extreme harshness and a great deal of callous brutality. The victims are conveyed in cattle trucks, stifling in summer, deadly cold in winter. Families are separated. Many die on the way. At the end of the interminable railway journey the poor wretches may have to march for miles over forest and steppe with insufficient food and water. In the case of the deportation of the Chechens, who had already suffered terribly for their resistance to the collectivization, the move was carried out as a military operation. Under cover of a special army exercise the valleys and mountainsides were filled with troops, who surrounded the villages and settlements, and then closed in, shooting to overcome resistance. This, however, was seen as a punitive operation against a rebellious and treacherous tribe; as a rule the people go quietly under police supervision, and their suffering is regarded as a sad but unavoidable necessity.

All this has nothing to do with forced labour as such,

seen as the equivalent of the tsarist *katorga:* it is a combination of direction of labour and compulsory resettle-
ment carried out in the crudest possible manner, but it is
something which the average Russian has come to take
almost for granted. His hold on his home base, as it were,
is precarious in the extreme. For example, there are at
least two million people now living in Moscow, and working too, who have no business to be there. In that fantastically overpopulated city one has to be registered officially
in order to obtain a flat, or a room, or a part of a room, or
a cellar, at the legal extremely moderate rental. But there
is work for far more people than the city will legally house,
even by Russian standards, where a whole room for a family and a share in a communal kitchen is the height of
bliss; and this means that people come in, unregistered,
and pay exorbitant premiums and rents for a share in the
home of somebody else. As I have said, there are at least
two million of these illegal residents in Moscow alone, and
all are liable to immediate expulsion if they are discovered. If they are lucky, they are sent to some new town in
the east which is short of people; if unlucky, to a labour
camp. This is the kind of thing which makes it altogether
impossible to determine the exact boundary between penal
forced labour and coercion in general. But when all allow-
ances are made, the number of prisoners sentenced to the
equivalent of the tsarist *katorga* is very great indeed. Instead of the thirty thousand of prerevolutionary days there
appear to be at least ten million, including the deportees
from the Baltic States (who are now, of course, Soviet citizens), Poland, Czechoslovakia, and the rest. In order to
appreciate this problem and see it in some form of perspective, it is necessary to look back at its history. For, like
every other aspect of Soviet life upon which we have

touched in these pages, this terrible and monstrous institution of large-scale forced labour was not planned by any
master mind. It simply grew.

Under the tsarist *katorga* system, political offenders and
common criminals were mixed up together in conditions
of intolerable harshness and squalor, their lives controlled
absolutely by irresponsible officials corrupted and demor-
alized by the power of life and death and by their remote-
ness from any centre of authority or civilization. The
katorga was described in its full horror by several tsarist
writers, notably Dostoevsky and Chekhov. These descrip-
tions physically sicken the English reader. Nevertheless, it
could be argued that the *katorga* differed from our own
penal servitude not in kind but only in degree.

Under the Bolsheviks there was going to be an end of
the *katorga*. Under the Soviet system the motives for crime
were to vanish, and with them crime itself. The criminal
was held to be the product of a ruinous environment, more
sinned against than sinning, and convicts inherited from
Nicholas II, and too far gone for immediate redemption,
were addressed with loving-kindness. On the other hand,
something had to be done with the active opponents of
the new system, who had to be put out of harm's way and,
if possible, reformed. So the corrective concentration
camps appeared. These were run, alas, not by Marxist the-
orists but by officers of the newly formed Cheka, who
turned out to be blood brothers of their late predecessors
of the Ochrana. Conditions in the new camps, notoriously
in the camps on the Solovetsky Islands in the White Sea,
rapidly equalled, then surpassed, in horror the camps described by Chekhov in *Sakhalin Island*. Russia was still
Russia, and now the whole country was in chaos, smitten
by famine and war: the prisoners were the first to die of
hunger and disease, and there was no question of wasting

good men to attend to them. Crime, far from dying out, increased fantastically and political offenders multiplied. It was against the principles of the early Soviet government to build new prisons, and thus the camps became over-crowded, even by Russian standards. All this was in full swing under the beneficent rule of Lenin, who, of course, had no idea of what was going on. He, like Nicholas before him, was too busy; and nobody ever told him. There was a grand attempt to reform the camps in 1923, and then the Bolsheviks gave up.

Already in 1918 the Soviet government had to decree that able-bodied prisoners were to be put to "tasks neces-sary for the state, tasks no more strenuous than those of unskilled workers," and for a time a great deal of stock was taken in the slogan "re-education through labour." This phrase, at least in its early days, was not entirely meaningless. One of the government's greatest problems was what to do with the millions of young hooligans, or-phans whose parents had been killed in the civil war and the famine, who ravaged the cities in droves, living on what they could get by robbery and murder. The worst of these hunted in packs, and there were periods in Moscow and Leningrad when to go out unaccompanied at night meant certain death at the hands of these ghastly children, who would pull their victim down by sheer weight of num-bers and batter him to death. The worst were shot out of hand; but those who were not too far gone were gradually rounded up and set to work under armed guard, and an unknown proportion were ultimately reclaimed as decent citizens. I myself have known men who started life as *bez-prisorny* and worked their way back to self-respect under the slave drivers of the Security Police. "Re-education through labour" had worked with them, though not at all on the wide scale suggested by Einstein's film *Turksib,*

which dealt with the construction of the Turkestan railway, one of the great testing grounds of the system. Those
who were salvaged were the exceptions. For the rest, prisoners continued to die of exhaustion and disease. Whole
camps would be wiped out by epidemics, or by simple starvation because supplies failed to arrive. There are records
of cases in the far north where not only all the prisoners
but also the whole prison staff were wiped out in the course
of a single winter. Crime continued to flourish and ever-
fresh waves of "politicals" poured into the camps—no
longer predominantly priests and bourgeois oppositionists
now, but revolutionaries who had taken the wrong turning at this or that invisible crossroads. As the first decade
wore on, the labour of these prisoners began to play a perceptible but still uncalculated part in the national economy. Then, fairly suddenly, with the first Five-Year Plan
and war to the death on the kulaks, involving the trans-
portation of some five million living souls, the whole problem of penal or corrective labour in the U.S.S.R. assumed
an entirely new complexion.

Until 1930 it could still be argued that, like the tsarist
katorga, Soviet forced labour was no more than penal servitude *à la russe.* The comparative severity of penal servitude in Russia reflected the comparative severity of ordinary life in Russia. The sickening aspects of the whole
institution reflected the difference between Russian and
English conceptions of the physically endurable, of the
powers of police and central government, of the probity
and responsibility of government officials. Soviet Russia
was also always short of food, often desperately short, and
there simply was not enough to feed the prisoners properly.
There was also the Russian idea that the "political" is
more wicked and dangerous than the common murderer,
or blackmailer, or thief, since the one injures society as a

whole whereas the other injures only individuals (this is a Russian, not a Bolshevik, conception). But with the huge influx of manpower from the villages of western Russia, the G.P.U., who now, in succession to the Cheka, had control of all prisoners, found itself in possession of a valuable asset. At first it was content to hire out its prisoners as cheap labour for local enterprises, much as the British government hired out German prisoners of war to British farmers, or D.P.s in Germany to German firms and municipalities. Later it began to plan its own enterprises. At first the government, in its official calculations, took no account of this forced labour. But in 1930 the new planning commissions were instructed "to incorporate the work performed by those deprived of liberty into the planned economy of the Five-Year Plan." To answer the new demand, the G.P.U. set up a special organization, known as GULAG, which to this day controls the whole immense network of labour camps—so that the GULAG chiefs in certain areas, notably the Kolyma goldfields, are in fact the governors of huge regions, controlling empires as large as a European country populated entirely by slaves, engineers and technicians living in exile, and their own staffs. And, as a rule, the great majority of camp guards are police who have themselves been exiled for offences against the regulations, now, by excess of zeal, trying to work their own passages back to freedom: their camp overseers are invariably taken, as in tsarist days, from among the convicted criminals, who, as I have said, are considered to be less reprehensible than the "politicals" whom they rule.

It should be pointed out that the chief M.V.D. officials in these areas are extremely powerful and gifted men. Mr. Wendell Willkie dined with one of them, whom he visualized simply as the governor of Magadan province (this being nothing else but a so-called "special area" administered entirely by the M.V.D.), on his tour of the Soviet Union. The first administrator of this area, a Mr. Rhein-gold Berzin, was shot on the charge that he was conspiring with a foreign power to secure the secession of the Kolyma region from the U.S.S.R. He was so powerful on his own ground that Moscow did not dare simply order his arrest. Instead, he was called to Moscow to receive the thanks of the government and a high decoration for his achievements in building up the terrible Dalstroy project, which cost innumerable lives. In the aeroplane which came to fetch him was a specially printed copy of *Izvestia* containing a bogus decree announcing his award. Berzin, any suspicions he had being completely lulled, gave a banquet to the incoming officials and afterwards entered the plane for Moscow, where he found himself taken prisoner at the point of a revolver. I retell this story, omitting a great deal of all but incredible detail, partly to emphasize the extraordinary power of these M.V.D. potentates, and partly to indicate the element of improvised high fantasy, more clumsily macabre than efficient, which runs through the Kremlin's actions.

The next stage in the development of the forced labour industry was the handing over to the G.P.U. (as the M.V.D. was known until 1938) of certain projects of the kind hitherto carried out by the relevant government departments, with or without the help of convict labour. It was up to the G.P.U. to carry out these assignments in its own way. It knew only one way. It set its own pace with the construction of the Baltic-White Sea Canal, which was completed in two years. At one time 250,000 prisoners, including engineers of the highest qualifications, were said to be employed on this project, which has been greatly admired as an example of Socialist enterprise. Since all the praise in the Soviet press went to Henry Yagoda, then head of the G.P.U., and afterwards executed during the great purge, nobody had any excuse at all for not realizing that this, among a hundred lesser projects, was an exclusively G.P.U. affair.

From that time the problem of the G.P.U. was no longer how to make the best use of its prisoners, but how to get more prisoners to carry out its projects. And that remains the problem of its successor, the M.V.D., today. Since 1931 forced labour in the U.S.S.R. has not been comparable with penal servitude as generally understood but rather has resembled in principle the slavery of vanished empires.

This is the general outline of the story as it has been generally understood by close students of Russia for a long time past. The Soviet government has not concealed the existence of forced labour, but only its extent and the conditions under which it is carried out. There have been frequent references in the Soviet press to good work done by prisoners. Mr. Molotov himself was explicit on the subject in the thirties, when the question of importing Russian timber cut by slave labour was raised by the British government. Indeed, there is no reason at all why forced labour in a mild degree should not exist, as the Soviet equivalent of Dartmoor. What matters is the scale and the motives behind it; and here, as in so many aspects of Russian life, the scale is such as to make a difference of degree between Russia and the West into a difference of kind.

To sum up, there seems hardly to have been a stage in the development of forced labour to its present monstrous proportions at which the head of the Soviet state could have said: thus far and no farther! The nature of the Bolshevik dictatorship combined with the nature of the Russian people, the peculiarities of Russian geography, the urgency of the industrial revolution, the hostile isolation of the Soviet Union, and the Russian tradition of arbitrary violence—all these converge with irresistible pressure. The counterrevolutionary opposition had to be corralled off and set to work; the apathetic, disillusioned, bread- and land-seeking masses had to be terrorized and coerced; the industrialization had to be forced through at a breakneck pace while corn needed to feed the people had to be exported to buy machines; everyone who stood in the way of the forced rationalization of the Soviet economy, above all the peasants resisting collectivization, had to be removed; new areas had to be opened up for gold and other metals and great constructional projects to be carried out—areas in which nobody would go to live of his own accord, even for high pay, areas where the winters are the coldest in the world and where ice lies just below the surface under the sweltering summer sun, turning thousands of square miles into a desolation of bogland where the mosquitoes shut out the light of the sun; the obvious organization to carry out these projects was the G.P.U., which thus developed a vested interest in prison labour; at the same time the commissars and industrial chiefs of all the ministers were crying out for cheap, expendable labour, and they got it from the G.P.U. Add to these pressures the insecurity of an unpopular régime, made more unpopular by its ruthlessness, a régime headed by Russians with their traditional obsession with security and by Bolsheviks who knew too much about conspiracy and what a few determined revolutionaries may do, a régime, moreover, desperately afraid of attack from the outside world. Who is to tell how many prisoners are taken for reasons of security, how many to make an example of idle workers, how many because the G.P.U. projects needed them? And who can possibly deny that the whole nightmare has become the total embodiment of Soviet muddle, improvisation, hand-to-mouth opportunism, defeating its own purpose and at the same time making it impossibly hard to end? In 1941, 14 per cent of the total productive output of the U.S.S.R. was supplied by the enterprises of the N.K.V.D. In 1941 the Soviet Union was barely solvent, with hardly enough food and clothing for its free workers. If Stalin, by decree, had suddenly opened his prison camps, the national economy would have fallen. This was not planned.

There are signs today that a very great effort is being made to reduce the forced-labour system. Increasingly, giant excavating machines replace the wretched slaves who dug canals with broken picks and carried the earth away on little stretchers. Increasingly the mines are being mechanized, while new towns go up in remote areas, attracting voluntary workers or those condemned to the milder forms of exile, thus reducing the need for prison labour. With the Russification of the Baltic States the M.V.D. exhausted its last major sources of slave labour. The delegate of the American Federation of Labor to the U.N. Economic and Social Council produced in 1950 a photostat document giving guidance to the M.V.D. in the Baltic States and listing as persons to be arrested and removed to forced labour in Russia the following categories of people:

Persons who have occupied prominent positions in the civil or communal service. Prominent members of the anti-Communist parties: Social Democrats, liberals. Small farmers. Active members of Jewish, Bund and Zionist organizations. Mystics, such as Freemasons and Theosophists. Industrialists, wholesale merchants, owners of large houses, shipowners, owners of hotels and restaurants, persons who have been in the diplomatic service, permanent representatives of foreign commercial firms, relatives of persons who have escaped abroad.

All these were taken, husbands separated from wives, and sent off to "the remote regions of Siberia" in the dreadful convoys described so movingly in *The Dark Side of the Moon*.

Unless the Kremlin proposes to conquer other lands, the M.V.D. can expect no more windfalls of this kind, and although the terror remains in Russia, and will remain, as the standard of living slowly climbs, as mechanization is substituted for hand labour, the total number of prisoners is bound to decline. They can still be obtained in a hundred and one unexpected ways, and in ways, still, characteristically mingling the needs of security with the need for cheap labour. A village gets up a petition to have its church reopened: twenty signatures make this legally possible, and twenty-three signatures are forthcoming; but the M.V.D. arrests four of the petitioners, so that the church remains closed and the labour force is richer. The *upravdom*, the official housemaster, of a large block of flats is told that his zeal in the Communist cause is suspected: he had better prove himself by discovering sedition in his block. So the *upravdom* carefully reports two or three individuals whom he does not like, or who have been caught in careless talk; and in the middle of the night they are taken away. A factory fails in its plan, or certain machines keep breaking down: there is a desperate hunt for scapegoats, and these, when decided on, are taken away. Throughout the whole Soviet Union there runs a crazy network of spies and informers. These may or may not be efficient in uncovering sedition; but they are certainly efficient in keeping it deeply underground—and in providing the M.V.D. with men to take away.

I have gone into the matter of forced labour in the Soviet Union at some length, not so much for its own sake as for what it tells us about the way things are done in

Russia. I have tried to show that it is not the deliberate creation of a malignant autocrat, but the outcome of a natural process stemming from the revolution. And it seems to me that the development of forced labour and police rule under the Soviet home office gives us an added insight into the way things are done by the Soviet foreign office, and offers, by analogy, additional evidence to contradict the idea that Soviet policy is really thought out at all—or, at least, that the general movement of Soviet policy bears any relation at all to anything that the Bolsheviks have ever tried to achieve—with the one great exception: the industrial revolution.

2

The Price of the Cold War

AFTER THE WAR most Russians believed that Stalin would relax his grip and ride them on a looser rein. They did not hope for much. Their economy was ruined and half European Russia was laid waste. They had been through a terrible time, and they had a terrible time ahead of them to rebuild with depleted strength and a catastrophic shortage of able-bodied men everything that had been destroyed. They were worn down with exhaustion, but they were ready to do this, each individual in what affected him most closely, if only they were left alone and if only some part of their Sisyphean labours could be returned to them as food, houses, pots and pans, clothes. It was more than the war that had afflicted them. Since 1914 the Russian people had lived in conditions of severe crisis. First war, then defeat and mutiny; then revolution, civil war, famine, and foreign intervention; then the cruelties of the collectivization and the rigours of the first two Five-Year Plans; then the brutal purges of the thirties; then, finally, the results of all their sacrifice and labour smashed to atoms by Hitler and his Germans. They needed, above all, rest and peace.

At first, Stalin did a great deal to encourage the belief that times would be a little easier. And although this may have been a trick to put the Russians in good heart for the ardours that lay ahead, there is plenty of evidence to support the idea that he, too, saw the necessity for relaxation. As far as the Great Russians were concerned, they now felt themselves a nation, taking pride and strength in their unity, as never before. Stalin, for all his past atrocities, had led them into a spectacular victory and become their symbol. In their newly found confidence they were ready to forget the past and tackle the unknown future, inspired by Stalin's confidence in them. The Ukraine and White Russia had their individuality at least symbolically acknowledged with the granting of technical national status within the U.S.S.R. With the cruel and total crushing of the rebellious Tartars of the Crimea and the Chechens and Ingushes of the Caucasus by the simple expedient of deleting their republics from the map of the Soviet Union and deporting them en masse to far Siberia in the wake of the Volga Germans, the Union had been strengthened and hotbeds of potential trouble cleared. By various heavy-handed expedients, returning soldiers and civilians believed to be infected with the virus of the West were effectively segregated and made impotent. The more unreliable elements of the western borderlands were either settled in Soviet Asia or sent, with hundreds of thousands of Polish, Latvian, Esthonian, and Lithuanian patriots, to the labour camps of the Russian interior. All this was done expeditiously and with a minimum of fuss. Ignoring the existence of some millions of captive wretches, Stalin could claim and believe that he ruled over a Soviet Union more united in patriotic submission to his will than, until the war, they had ever seemed likely to be. He had only one possible rival in the popular imagination, and that was Marshal Zhukov, the hero of the great offensives. But Marshal Zhukov, together with his great comrades in arms, was quietly put in cold storage. Stalin, the victorious leader, assumed the title "Generalissimo," and henceforward nobody was ever allowed to remember that there had been any supreme command but him. While Zhukov and his colleagues, forbidden Moscow except when invited for special consultations, were relegated to the great strategic garrisons in the provincial borderlands, the history of the war was already being rewritten, again and again rewritten, until, today, the story of Stalingrad is told with no single reference to the great commander in chief.

All the signs were that Russia was withdrawing from the world in order to lick her own wounds. The Iron Curtain in face of the West was finally locked by the inconspicuous and unprecedented decree formally forbidding marriage between Soviet citizens and foreigners. That was in March 1947. The Zhdanov purge to free the arts of all foreign influences got into its stride in the autumn of 1946, and cosmopolitanism and formalism became the deadly sins. Very soon the government researchers emerged with their curious findings which set off the great wave of Russian claims to every invention under the sun, from penicillin to the electric light. Soviet man was exalted as the highest type of being, and Soviet patriotism as the summit of human nobility. At the same time there were notable relaxations on the part of the Kremlin. The abolition of the death penalty in May 1947 was a great symbolic act. The death penalty is, and always has been, regarded in Russia with peculiar horror, although this may seem strange in a country where life is held so cheap, where offenders are liquidated with the greatest of ease, and where millions are condemned in the labour camps to what is all too often no more than a living death. Its abolition was for Russians the highlight of a trend towards benevolent paternalism, itself accompanied by a perceptible move towards decentralization of administration, which was something quite new in the Soviet Union. The elaborate purge of the arts and the grossly inflated party was accompanied by much sound and fury, but very few people were seriously hurt. Prokofiev's two ballets, *Cinderella* and *Romeo and Juliet,* continued in the Moscow repertoire after the vicious onslaught of the Zhdanov committee. Even Zoschenko, the Leningrad satirist, and the archetype of everything that the Soviet writer of the future was not to be, was sentenced only to sit at home and atone for his sins by writing a novel about partisans (incidentally, that novel, which would resemble nothing so much as a tract by Mr. Evelyn Waugh about the Boy Scout movement, has never appeared). There was one object, and one object only, in this purification of the arts: to give the Russian people confidence in themselves and their special ability to mould the forces of nature to their needs. It was as if Mr. Smiles had been made minister of culture and propaganda in the cabinet of Lord Palmerston. But there was no Mr. Smiles in Russia, which is naturally allergic to the idea of self-improvement; instead there was only a committee of energetic but bewildered literary sycophants, relying on mass repetition of a few simple lies to make up for their lack of ideas.

When the Zhdanov purge was in full swing I asked a group of Russian writers what it was all about. "Zoschenko . . . !" they all replied, "Zoschenko—Zoschenko—Zoschenko . . . !" And then each except one, who has since suffered eclipse himself, made an individual little speech, watching his colleagues out of the corner of his eye, explaining that Zoschenko was abhorred because, instead of fighting, instead even of writing patriotic verses, he had gone on with his defeatist nonsense, sitting among the orange groves of Tashkent while his countrymen bled and died for him, turning out stories which compared the Soviet Union with a zoo. I said, all right; that accounted for Zoschenko. But what interested me very much more was the case of Madame Akhmatova, who was a woman of advanced age, who had never compared a commissar to a monkey, who had done nothing at all but quietly produce her exquisite verses. What had *she* been expected to do in the war? And why, if she had disgraced herself by not writing war poetry, had the elderly Mikhail Prishvin, the most beautiful writer in Russia, with his stories of the forest and the steppe, not been attacked as well? What had *he* done in the war? There was a long silence, which was suddenly broken by a charming, middle-aged writer of patriotic sailors' songs. Everybody stared apprehensively at this gentleman, who looked apprehensive himself, but said with resolution, "I think I can give the gentleman the answer in two words." Everybody gasped, but the speaker continued boldly, "The answer is this: Mr. Prishvin writes about animals and birds, and loves them. He is therefore harmless. But Madame Akhmatova writes about human beings, and does not love them. This is not harmless." Everybody burst out laughing, and the writer of sailors' songs sat down beaming with satisfaction and relief. And in fact he had given a good answer. For the purge of the arts had nothing to do with the war records of Soviet writers and artists, or even with their politics. On the one hand, it was designed to kill foreign influence. But the chief reason for fearing foreign influence (and this lay behind all the talk about cosmopolitanism and formalism) was because it carried the virus of self-questioning—in a word, of pessimism. The Russians, at the best of times, are all too easily the prey of pessimism. But once a few dozen Russian artists began to question themselves, their destiny, the meaning of life, and the future of the human race— then good-bye to the Five-Year Plan. . . . It was as simple as that—and, at heart, as harmless.

And this, by Russian standards, harmlessness was a feature of all the paternal activities of the first two years after the war. Even the vigorous campaign, for example, to restore the collective farms to their pristine rigidity and to clean up the abuses which had developed and flourished during the war was at first conducted, again by Stalinist standards, with remarkable leniency. The emphasis throughout was on sorrow rather than anger. Collective directors found guilty, as thousands of them were, of selling communal property to individuals or, for a consideration, granting dispensations from collective work, were removed from their posts and degraded, but no more. At the same time various governmental actions suggested that the Kremlin was developing a greater confidence in the ability of its local party and government bodies to run their own affairs. Towards the end of 1947 it looked very much as though Stalin had come to the conclusion that in the Communist Party of the Soviet Union he had succeeded in building up a class of men and women orthodox to the point at which acceptance of certain principles was so instinctive that superficial deviations no longer mattered, men and women thus fit to act on their own under the most general supervision from above.

Then, quite suddenly, the whole liberalizing trend was stopped and almost at once the process went into reverse. This was at the end of 1947; and for the next two years the tightening of the central power continued, ever more convulsively, until as its climax in January 1950 the death penalty was restored. Today the Kremlin bears more heavily (though less bloodily than in the past) on the lives of the Russian masses than ever before. And all this, as far as it may be seen, represents the price the people of the Soviet Union are paying for the waging of the Cold War. Oppressed, as we are, by the burden of our own sacrifices in this tragicomic struggle, we overlook the fact that the other side must also pay. But Stalin knows all about that.

3

The Sinews of War

THE SOVIET UNION has a population verging on two hundred million, four times the population of Great Britain, a third as much again as the population of the United States. It occupies one-sixth of all the land in the world. It has thousands of square miles of the most fertile land in the world. It disposes of astronomical reserves of coal, iron, nonferrous metals, and oil. It has a standing army, including short-term conscripts, of nearly three million men. It is ruled by men who have no scruples, believe in the supremacy of force, and control a highly organized fifth column in every country in the world with the single exception of Switzerland. These are the facts which have hypnotized us into the belief that the Soviet Union is the greatest power in the world and reduced us to a state of hysteria. Let us look at these facts from the other side of the hill.

A few figures:

With all its great population the Soviet Union was

scheduled to produce in 1950 only 250 million tons of coal, as against Britain's 200 million and America's 700 million tons. The comparative figures for steel are the Soviet Union's 25 million tons as against Britain's 15 million tons and America's 90 million tons. The oil production of the Soviet Union for 1950 was to be some 35 million tons, as against America's 250 million tons. So much for heavy industry.

In agriculture, with a greatly increased population, and notwithstanding the addition to the Soviet Union of all the Baltic States, part of East Prussia, the Polish Ukraine, and a number of smaller items, including Moldavia and Bessarabia, the grain production in 1950 barely exceeded the 1940 level of grain production; and in 1940 the total still lagged behind the precollectivization production of 1928. In 1950 there were some 600,000 tractors in use in the Soviet Union, as against 260,000 in Britain and more than 3,000,000 in the United States. When it comes to motor transport for agricultural purposes, the total number of trucks and lorries delivered in the Soviet Union for all purposes was 64,000, in America more than 2,000,000.

I have fought shy of figures in this book; but it seems to me that the assortment cited here indicates more clearly than anything else the immense discrepancy between the Soviet potential and the Soviet reality. It indicates that in spite of its vast area and unlimited resources, the productivity of Soviet Russia is so low that it has needed its four-to-one superiority in manpower to surpass the industrial production of Great Britain, and that it has no hope at all of catching up with the United States for many decades to come.

For the purposes of the present argument it is not necessary to inquire into the reasons for this low level of productivity (these have already been indicated very sketchily earlier in the book); all we are concerned with now is the simple fact. It is a fact which conditions the outlook of Stalin on the outside world, and it is a fact which dominates his whole domestic policy. The effort to attain and sustain this comparatively modest output, and to keep it rising, is symbolized by the Five-Year Plans, which engage the greater part of the energies of government and people and condemn the Russian masses to a bare subsistence level of existence in conditions of extreme harshness and privation.

The Soviet government is acutely aware of the low level of output per head. In 1939 Stalin himself put the problem:

In what respects are we lagging behind? We are lagging economically as regards the volume of our industrial output per head of population. In 1938 we produced about 15 million tons of pig iron; Great Britain produced 7 million tons. It might seem from this that we are better off than Great Britain. But if we divide the number of tons by the total populations, we shall find that the output of pig iron per head of population in 1938 was 145 kilograms in Great Britain and only 87 kilograms in the U.S.S.R. Or, further, if Great Britain produced 10 million eight hundred thousand tons of steel and about 29 billion kilowatt-hours of electricity, whereas the U.S.S.R. produced 18 million tons of steel and over 39 billion kilowatt-hours of electricity, it might seem that we are better off than Great Britain. But if we divide this number of tons and kilowatt-hours by the total populations, we shall find in 1938 in Great Britain the output of steel per head of population was 226 kilograms, and of electricity 620 kilowatt-hours, whereas in the U.S.S.R. the output per head of population was only 107 kilograms of steel and of electricity only 223 kilowatt-hours. . . . Thus, in order to outstrip Britain economically in the production of pig iron, which in 1938 amounted in that country to 7 million tons, we must increase our annual output of pig iron to 25 million tons.

This the Soviet Union has not yet done. The target for pig iron in 1950 was 19.5 million tons. And meanwhile Britain had increased her 7 million tons to 10 million tons.

Production statistics are not enough, however. In spite of the gigantic efforts made by the Soviet Union and the remarkable recovery since the war (steel production in 1938 was 18 million tons; in 1945, 9 million tons; in 1950, 25 million tons), it is clear from these figures that the Russians are far less well equipped than the British, to say nothing of the Americans. On the other hand, every million tons of steel in Soviet Russia contributes far more to the sinews of heavy industrial development and war than a million tons in Britain or America. This is because in the Soviet Union only the barest minimum is diverted to improving the amenities of life from the provision of capital equipment, machinery, arms, and food and housing of the most elementary kind. In Britain, even in her present meagre circumstances, and far more in America, a great proportion of the total annual production goes to maintain a domestic standard of living undreamed of in the Soviet Union. And this helps to cancel out the advantage of the West in possessing a highly developed industrial economy in full running order.

Nevertheless, when the Kremlin looks at America it sees an annual production of 90 million tons of steel produced without strain and devoted to the improvement and enrichment of an economy already functioning in top gear. None of this steel is required for reconstruction programmes; almost all of it can be diverted at a moment's notice to the manufacture of armaments and munitions, which already include the largest navy in the world as well as the atomic bomb. To this gigantic output the Kremlin can oppose from Soviet sources rather more than one ton of steel to every four. And this is produced by straining every nerve and keeping down the standard of living at a dangerously low level. For the time being, the bulk of the Kremlin's steel is required for reconstructing a ruined economy which, compared with the American economy, was rudimentary even before it was ruined.

In February 1946 Stalin proclaimed the highest recorded ambition of the Soviet planners, the trebling of the prewar output. It was a tremendous call to sacrifice, because before the prewar output could be increased it first had to be restored, and that was going to take four years of the first Five-Year Plan. And it was in this speech that Stalin gave the first indication that with the defeat of Germany the Russians could not hope for everlasting peace:

> We must achieve a situation whereby our industry is able to produce each year up to 50 million tons of pig iron, up to 60 million tons of steel, up to 500 million tons of coal, and up to 60 million tons of oil. Only under such conditions can we regard our country as guaranteed against any accidents. This, I think, will require perhaps three more Five-Year Plans, if not more.

A great deal has happened since those brave words were spoken. Then, at the beginning of 1946, Stalin still expected to receive heavy reparations from Germany and still hoped for American credits. The Cold War can have been nothing more than a wild dream of the more doctrinaire and arrogant members of the Central Committee. When, a year and a half later, the great decision was taken, it added greatly to the burden. A greater proportion of the total resources had to be earmarked for rearmament and, in addition, the shift of the Soviet Union's centre of gravity from the industrial and agricultural area of the Ukraine to the Urals and beyond had to be accelerated greatly for reasons of security.

At the same time, those truly heroic figures, which even when they were first conceived admitted the vast superiority of American production for fifteen years ahead, were themselves made to look ridiculous. Britain alone expanded her production to an extent which in 1946 must have seemed impossible to the Soviet observers of an economy which they believed was steadily declining. Her 11 million tons of steel in 1938 has now increased to 16 million. New industries have been developed throughout the British Empire. But what has made nonsense of the Soviet ambition has been the mobilization of American industry to fight the Cold War. In three years' time, for example, the present American steel capacity is to be expanded by an amount greater in itself than the total British steel capacity, or about two-thirds of the entire Soviet capacity—and this on top of the present production of 90 million tons. During the next three years America is to spend five times the entire British national income on her defence effort. And so on. And the fantastic aspect of the whole enterprise is that this colossal output is reckoned to be only a third of what America could produce in time of war. It is to this that Stalin has been brought by Soviet diplomacy in five short years.

A great power cannot rest on steel alone. It also needs

food. Food in Russia, for the masses, still means bread, black or white, wheat or rye, and buckwheat porridge, with sunflower oil for fat. Meat, milk, butter, fish, fresh vegetables, are extras. In 1949 it was officially stated that the output of grain and potatoes had at last surpassed the prewar level. But from a careful study of the Soviet press alone it can be demonstrated that this claim was untrue: the official returns of the 1949 harvest were afterwards, in district after district, found to have been inflated by falsification to a greater or less degree, later publicly exposed; but the returns were never publicly corrected. Dr. Naun Jasny, in his monumental book on Soviet agriculture, has proved, conclusively to my mind, what I had always suspected, namely, that the official crop statistics have been consistently overestimated since the early days of the collectivization (since the early thirties, that is) by something like 20 per cent. This has been done by the simple process of abandoning the old and accurate method of computation based on the amount of grain actually harvested and stored in favour of the practice of estimating the weight of the crop in the field. The same sort of thing is done in industry, too.

But even allowing the official figures of the Central Statistical Bureau, the equalling of the prewar yield in 1949 is not an impressive performance. In the last three years before the war there was less grain available per head of population than in 1928, on the eve of the collectivization. Since 1938 the population of the Soviet Union, in spite of the tremendous wartime losses, is believed to have increased by something like thirty millions, partly owing to the very high birth rate, partly owing to the new blood brought by the populations of the annexed territories. At the same time, these territories have added very considerably to the area of land under cultivation.

None of these things is mentioned in the Soviet statistics. So that when Mr. Benediktov, the extremely gifted minister for agriculture, proudly announces that his 1949 production has surpassed prewar production, what he is really saying is this: According to the returns of the Central Statistical Bureau, which I know to be exaggerated by perhaps 20 per cent, the 1949 production of basic foodstuffs in the Soviet Union *plus* the three Baltic States, Lithuania, Esthonia and Latvia, *plus* a slice of East Prussia, *plus* the Polish Ukraine and the Transcarpathian Ukraine, *plus* Moldavia and Bessarabia, has just surpassed the 1940 production of basic foodstuffs for the Soviet Union without these additions, and the allowance *per capita* is thus considerably lower than it was in 1940, and lower still than it was in 1928, which itself (we have not mentioned this before) had just about reached the 1914 level.

While we are on the subject of Soviet statistics (and the manœuvres outlined above are characteristic of the whole), there is one other aspect which has no part in what they tell us. This is that the amount and variety and quality of food which was adequate for the slow, largely illiterate, three-parts peasant population of 1928 is not by any means adequate for the 1949 population with its vastly increased proportion of individuals working with their brains and mechanical skills. These need more than a flat and heavy diet of bread and potatoes if they are to do the work required of them.

These are the figures behind the impressions I set down in an earlier chapter about the mood of Russia in 1947. They are the figures which the leaders of the Communist Party are straining every nerve to improve. They are the figures which make it impossible for Stalin to conduct a Cold War against the West without driving the people almost beyond their endurance for the second time in twenty years, and at the very moment when they had allowed themselves to believe that they could at last relax. We can finish with figures now, but in contemplating the mighty armed façade they should never be out of our minds.

4

Faster, Faster!

IN 1941 THE SOVIET UNION was all but defeated by Germany. Stalin knows this. On the part of a nation of 180 millions which for the previous twelve years had put almost the whole of its energies and substance into preparing for defensive war, this was nothing less than a disgraceful performance. Stalin knows this too. He also knows the reason for it. Indeed, he expected it to happen, which is why he went to extreme lengths to placate the Nazi beast—and then, by the ineptitude of his diplomacy (or Mr. Molotov's), goaded it into attacking sooner than it would have done if left to itself. For I think that a study of the relevant documents leaves very little doubt that although a Hitler victorious over England would sooner or later have gone for the Ukraine, what set him off in 1941 was the almost claustrophobic feeling of being crowded and pushed about induced in him by Soviet pressure in the matter of Bessarabia, pressure which was the outcome of an obsession with security to the point of mania which prevented the Kremlin from leaving well alone. The more it changes the more it is the same. . . . Stalin, alas, does *not* know this.

Stalin knew that there would be trouble if Hitler invaded Russia because he had driven his people too hard, and above all in those vulnerable and partly alien borderlands in which dislike of Moscow rule will never die. In fact, when the Nazis invaded White Russia and the Ukraine they were welcomed as liberators from the Moscow tyranny. The people did not merely salute their conquerors with bread and salt; they took sides against the Red Army. I am not talking now about the active Ukrainian separatists, who deserted to the Germans and later served under General Vlassov, who himself deserted after his heroic defence of Moscow; I am talking about the ordinary villagers. And I am not citing the evidence of refugees and deserters. I am citing the evidence of serving soldiers of the Red Army who were appalled at the things the villagers did to them as they tried to fight rearguard actions with whole formations of their comrades throwing down their arms on either flank. For the curious thing about this collapse of the Red Army was that some formations fought like lions, while others did not fight at all. Even General Vlassov, who was hanged as a traitor, fought like a lion in front of Moscow before he changed sides.

What altered the whole picture was the behaviour of the Germans who, in a manner now familiar to us all, proceeded to demonstrate beyond all doubt that they were worse than the Communists and the N.K.V.D. What lost the war with Russia for Germany was the policy of the ineffable Herr Rosenberg, who demanded the use of fire and terror against the Russian population, and the remarkable ease with which large numbers of Germans were found who were pleased to carry out this policy. (What, one sometimes wonders, are they doing now? . . .) So the Ukraine and White Russia began to fight back as partisans. The terrible frosts of the early winter caught the Germans unprepared as they overreached themselves, but so very slightly, before the gates of Moscow (as Rommel was to overreach himself, also very slightly, in face of Cairo later in the war), and by now the Red Army was fighting back hard and Moscow was saved. But the same sort of thing happened all over again in 1942 at Rostov—until the Russians in the south learned their lesson too, and fought back at Stalingrad. On both occasions it was touch and go; and it was touch and go because the people had had enough of Stalin.

And now the whole tragic business is being repeated. Behind the great show of benevolent paternalism on the part of Stalin there lay a great disturbance of mind. He had the memory of what had happened in 1941 and 1942; he had the memory of the peasant women in the unscathed areas behind Moscow and Voronezh who, in that autumn of 1941, had left the crops to rot in the fields rather than harvest them for him; he had the memory of total demoralization of the Red Army on the Southern Front, expressing itself above all in self-inflicted wounds, so that a special branch of the N.K.V.D. had had to be formed, known as SMERSH, or Death to Traitors, to watch the fighting army, including its party organizers. He had the memory of Moscow in October 1941, when, after the partial evacuation of officialdom to Kuibyshev, the N.K.V.D. had broken down and burned their dossiers. Party officials had fled in droves to the remotest parts of Russia, taking the party funds with them. And the people of Moscow had risen and looted shops and offices—a rot which he himself had checked by suddenly appearing like a portent in the great hall of the Mayakovsky Station of the underground, to deliver his rallying speech for the twenty-third anniversary of the revolution.

He had all these memories, and many more besides, memories of a great nation breaking down because they had been driven to the breaking point; and he was faced with new dangers, above all the contagion from the West brought by the returning millions. And so he told the people of Russia that they were wonderful, which was true, and that he trusted them, which was not true, and that, although they must still work much harder than they liked, he would see that the old rigours were relaxed for them, which, as I have said, he probably hoped would be true.

But things had gone too far. We have seen how the system of forced labour had gone too far to be suddenly reversed; and so it has been with the Stalinist system as a whole. The first crack appeared with the great drought of 1946, a piece of wretched bad luck. Stalin, having got away with innumerable sins, was now being punished for something that was not his fault. For punished he was. He had promised, with the utmost confidence, the end of bread rationing for the winter of 1946; and that had to be postponed another year. It created a bad impression, and already the N.K.V.D. was functioning with its pristine energy to put down the grumblers and resisters. In the Polish Ukraine there was a state of war between the Soviet army and the remnants of the anti-Soviet Ukrainian armies, and between the N.K.V.D. and the peasants, who were resisting being collectivized, as their Soviet brothers had resisted twenty years before them. Reports were coming in from all over the Soviet Union that the breakdown of collectivization was more radical than anyone had thought, and that Mr. Andreyev's campaign was proving inadequate to deal with it: the food simply was not coming into the towns, and what did come in came in illegally, not only on the black market but as a result of the most complicated barter deals between individual factories and individual farms; so that the factories were ruining the Plan by making articles for the peasants instead of for the Centre. All this would have been bad enough without the great drought; but the great drought meant near famine and the consequent falling off of industrial production, so that a vicious circle was set up. In the winter of 1947, for example, there were organized bread riots in Kharkov and elsewhere, and many were killed in street fighting before the N.K.V.D. at last put the rioters down.

It was a vicious circle. The peasants would not produce enough food for the towns, preferring to neglect the collective work and labour on their private plots to sell on the free market at inflated prices; the towns, hungry and weary, produced fewer goods for the countryside, which grew increasingly disgruntled. And on top of this the artificially engineered war scare had the reverse of the effect intended: it made the people shrug their shoulders in despair.

This fills out the background to my impressions of 1947, already recorded, on the eve of Stalin's terrible decision to challenge the West and accelerate the breakdown of its economy—not, I am convinced, because he wanted to conquer the West (he had enough on his plate already: he was having great difficulty with the people in his existing zone of influence, who stretched his repressive apparatus to the limit), but in order to gain time, after one more short, convulsive effort, to build up the Soviet Union and his protective zone at leisure. If he could not raise the standard of living in Russia to the level of the West, he could at least reduce the standard of living of the West and so destroy its gravitational pull as well as incapacitate it as a military threat.

He has failed.

Within eighteen months of the beginning of E.R.P. the productive powers of Western Europe had been restored to their prewar level; while by his inept foreign policy, and above all the sanctioning of the attack on South Korea, Stalin has succeeded only in driving America into a radical expansion of her economy, based on a vast rearmament programme. As a result of this, the Kremlin has not only ranged against itself all the physical might outlined in the preceding chapter, but it has also removed all danger for some time to come of the catastrophic American slump upon which it had pinned its hope. At the same time, and in direct contrast to the returning prosperity of Western Europe, the People's Democracies in the East are being increasingly impoverished by the incessant drain of their substance into the Soviet Union, and instead of the belt of friendly nations working eagerly towards their own brands of socialism and linked by bonds of trade, self-interest, and genuine Slav feeling with their great neighbour, all the Kremlin can now lay claim to is a hotbed of present trouble and potential disaster precariously held down by the threat of Soviet might, reinforced by the fear of an avenging Germany.

Indeed, the only assets which now remain to the Kremlin, apart from the size, potential richness, and geographical position of the Soviet Union, are six in number. First, the bewilderment and the hatred of war and injustice of the peoples of the West; second, the progress of communism in Asia, allied as it is with the profound revulsion of the traditional underdog against all alien rule; third, the existence of a disciplined fifth column in every country of the West, disguised from its members as a branch of the Communist Party and from outsiders as a humanitarian revolutionary movement; fourth, the immediate striking power of the Soviet Army; fifth, the ignorance and powers of endurance of the Russian people; sixth, its own absolute lack of scruple.

The bewilderment of the peoples of the West is a matter which should be under our own control: it exists at the moment and is being powerfully exploited by the Kremlin, above all through the fraudulent peace campaign, but there is no reason why it should exist and we have the power to put an end to it ourselves. The progress of communism in Asia is certainly not a matter under our control, although we can do a great deal to check it. But it is scarcely more under the Kremlin's control than it is under our own. The Kremlin did not start that forest fire, although it pours oil on the flames; and it certainly cannot hope to control its ultimate direction. It is commonly supposed to derive great comfort from the revolution in China. This revolution will stand or fall by the success or failure of Mao Tse-tung in stabilizing that chaotic land and turning it into a coherent power. Yet for Russia the idea of a strong and unified China standing against her longest and most vulnerable land frontier must be today, as it has been for the last hundred years, a nightmare of the most vivid kind. No matter how well it may suit the Chinese Communists for the time being to profess loyalty to the Soviet Union and to take a leaf out of Stalin's book in their attempt to create regimented power and unity from chaos, the Kremlin must know very well that this can at best be only a temporary and tactical loyalty, that the Chinese dislike the Russians no less than other Europeans (it is we, not the Chinese, who make the mistake of thinking of the Russians as semi-orientals), and that to Stalin and his government who, in face of the Japanese threat, deliberately sacrificed the Chinese Communists for so many years to Chiang Kai-shek, they owe no loyalty and gratitude but only hatred and contempt. It is safe to say that sooner or later Stalin will be forced either to disrupt the Chinese Communist Party, preferably from within, or else to stand by apprehensively and watch the new China develop along her own lines. This does not alter the fact that for some time to come the appeal of the Communist movement, as symbolized by Stalin or Mao Tse-tung, or both, will continue to play havoc with American, British, Dutch, and French interests in Asia. But it does bear very closely on the question of the Soviet Union's imperialist pretensions. China is no more a part of the Soviet Union's sphere of influence than Great Britain and America were part of it during the Second World War. The two are allies of convenience. And Stalin would have no scruple at all in turning a Communist Japan loose on a Communist China if he thought that by so doing he would benefit from their mutual exhaustion. Mao Tse-tung must know this as well as we do. At the moment he is more afraid of an Americanized Japan.

The existence of a disciplined fifth column in all non-Communist countries is a powerful asset only partly under the Kremlin's control. Its effectiveness depends on matters under our own control. Its existence depends on the ability of the Kremlin to continue duping its members. Already there are signs of some disintegration from within, as key members, belatedly awakened to the fate in store for them and their faith should they ever succeed in carrying out a revolution in their own countries, sadly gather the courage to resign: their fate, of course, would be the fate of Rajk of Hungary, Kostov of Bulgaria, Clementis of Czechoslovakia, Gomulka of Poland, and of a host of smaller figures in the satellites, who have not been content that their party and their country should be degraded to the position of a mindless tool of Russian imperialism.

The remaining three assets—the immediate striking power of the Soviet army, the ignorance and capacity for endurance of the Russian people, and the unscrupulousness of the Soviet government—are the only three which by any stretch of imagination can be said to be wholly under the Kremlin's control. Even then, the first two are relative; only the third is absolute.

The power of the Soviet army is relative because it derives from our present weakness. The endurance of the Russian people is relative because it is not unlimited. The unscrupulousness of the Politburo is absolute, but without adequate instruments to carry out its will—in the way of brains and force—it is impotent. If anybody after reading so far is still impressed by the power and subtlety of Stalin's brain as manifested in Soviet diplomacy, I can only say I am sorry. We are now considering the force.

The sinews of war we have already looked at. There remain the strength of the armed forces as such and the morale of the people who stand behind the army.

On paper the Soviet army is overwhelming. Nobody knows its real strength; but it is commonly accepted now that it consists of something under three million men (2,800,000 is the figure usually given to make our flesh creep) and has in being 175 divisions. I myself do not believe that the Kremlin at this moment disposes of 175 complete divisions on a war footing, because I do not believe that there are enough senior N.C.O.s and middle-grade staff officers (majors and colonels) to staff all these divisions and at the same time attend to the training of the great mass of short-term conscripts, which includes a high proportion of scarcely literate young peasants. The demand for skilled men of this kind is far larger than the supply. Industry screams for them and does not get them. During the discussion of the 1950 budget in the Supreme Soviet, minister after minister, castigated for shortfalls in production, indicted the Ministry of Higher Education and the Ministry of Labour Reserves for their continued failure to produce in sufficient numbers skilled overseers and technicians. It was not the fault of the wretched scapegoats: the material did not exist.

In an earlier chapter, dealing with my impressions of Russia in 1947, I mentioned the fact that most individuals in the white-collar classes were doing two or three separate jobs and working up to eighteen hours a day in order to earn sufficient roubles to supplement their rations with purchases in the free "commercial shops." They were able to do this only because the demand for their skill was so great. During the war my own opposite number, a middle-grade staff officer in the Soviet War Office, had to divide his time between three distinct appointments: he was a G.S.O.1 on the General Staff, and every week he spent three or four days supervising analogous departments at Army Group and Army Headquarters in the field. And so it is with every ministry. There is only one organization in the Soviet Union which is not desperately short of skilled and responsible leaders, and that is the combined M.V.D. and M.G.B., which between them, it is believed, account for over a million men. These, though armed and equipped to form a complete standing army, are not used to fight. During the war there were some 600,000 N.K.V.D. troops in Russia, but they were never, even in the most desperate moments, used to fight the Germans. Their job was at home.

But even allowing the official Western estimate of 175 divisions to be correct, what sort of force does this make?

In the first place, it has to be remembered that the Soviet division is a small one. It has some 10,000 men, or about half the number of the ordinary British division; so that 175 Soviet divisions are the equivalent of some 90 British or American divisions. This is still a great many, but is it, seen from the Kremlin, as excessive as it seems to us in the West?

Before the 1914 war, Russia had a regular army of over a million men. At this time Germany had 500,000 and France 600,000. Since then the population of the area covered by the Soviet Union has been nearly doubled, so that, other things being equal, we should expect a corresponding increase in the army. Other things, of course, are not equal: we in the West have been trying to do without armies, while the Russians have clung to theirs. But at least it is clear that an army of 2,800,000, including short-term conscripts, is not the product of a great rearmament drive. Its overwhelming size is bound up with the overwhelming size of the Soviet Union, which occupies one-sixth of all the land in the world and has land frontiers of inordinate length and extreme vulnerability. These frontiers, particularly the frontier with China, cannot possibly be fortified along their whole length; but they call for spaced concentrations of troops all round the vast perimeter. The size of the problem from the point of view of the Soviet General Staff is clearly indicated by the present breakdown of the Soviet forces into self-contained armies, each, as far as is possible, drawing its supplies from industrial areas in its immediate rear. There are six of these commands: the Northern Army, based on Leningrad; the Western Army, based on Minsk; the Southern Army, based on Odessa; the Caucasian Army, based on Tiflis; the Turkestan Army, based on Tashkent and Frunze; the Far Eastern Army, based on Chita and Vladivostok. The reputed 175 divisions, equal to 90 of ours, have to be shared out between these widely spaced commands, leaving a strong force over for Germany and Austria. We talk very glibly about the advantages of interior lines; and certainly Hitler, sitting in Berlin, was able to make the most of these advantages during the last war. But interior lines in the Soviet Union are another matter. With those immense distances, linked by still inadequate railways and next to no good roads, the task of switching a couple of divisions from one front to another is not an easy one; and while to us the outline of the Soviet Union on the map represents a vast area of hidden menace, from which thrusting columns may debouch at any point, to Moscow that same outline represents a thin red line, impossible to defend, which may be pierced at any point.

As for the quality and fighting power of the Soviet divisions, they are extremely mixed. The real strength of the Soviet army as an attacking force is not, as most people seem to think, in its foot soldiers, but in its tanks and artillery, including special rocket devices of the *Katusha* kind. There are a great many tanks of the kind used during the last war, the medium T34s, some of them equipped with new and bigger guns. In addition there are a number of heavy Joseph Stalin IIIs, which strike terror into the hearts of Western commentators. But these are of little use in a break-through, since they can carry only a very small number of rounds for their 122 mm. guns; and the Soviet supply system is such that what a tank does not carry itself it is unlikely to get when most wanted. These Joseph Stalin IIIs are first class in defence or in a slow, grinding advance; but we are not invited to consider the Soviet army in defence: what we are asked to consider is a headlong rush through Europe.

There is only one way of carrying out a fast-moving

attack, and that is by the use of fast-moving troops, perfectly coordinated. Thus, if such an attack is what we expect, we must rule out of the critical action at least two-thirds of the Soviet army as it now is, which reduces its numbers to more manageable proportions. The great mass of the Soviet infantry is quite incapable of taking part in a Blitzkrieg. Even those infantry divisions which are said to be mechanized do not as a rule allocate motor transport permanently and on a fixed scale to regiments and battalions, as in Western armies, but keep the transport in a divisional pool, with its own company of drivers. This is due not only to the shortage of motor vehicles, already indicated in an earlier chapter, but also to the fact that in the average Soviet infantry battalion there are very few men capable of the simple care and maintenance of motor vehicles. For the rest, the infantry rely mainly on horse-drawn transport. The columns on the move, straggling over the countryside with their little wooden carts like large pig troughs on spidery wheels, are, apart from the armament of the soldiers, indistinguishable in appearance and scarcely distinguishable in character from their ancestors of the Napoleonic Wars. In connection with motor transport, it should be added that the supply of trucks and other motor vehicles from America was far and away the most important item in the military aid to Russia provided by the Western Allies. At the time of the Stalingrad envelopment it may, indeed, have been a decisive item. Further, as recently as 1947, among all the military transport which was still on the roads, I myself did not see one single truck, apart from a handful of dilapidated prewar vans, which was not either American or British or captured German. The spares for these must now be running low.

In a long, slogging advance, the best of the infantry are

obviously magnificent material. With the sappers, who bridge great rivers with trees cut down on the spot, they are remarkable for making bricks without straw. They will live on the country and go without food, when there is none, for days on end. They are not cluttered up with the extravagant administrative tail which distinguishes the modern mechanized army of the West. For officers below the rank of major no records are kept, which does away with a great deal of paper work. When supplies are brought up to the line they do not come in response to elaborate indents from individual units and formations: base simply sends up what it has in the way of stores in the general direction of the front, and the convoys are intercepted and broken up and individual trucks directed to those units which seem to need the stores most urgently. When a Russian soldier goes away to war, he simply goes; and that is the end of him as far as his family is concerned, unless once in a way he gets a letter through, or until he turns up on leave, or until one of his comrades turns up to say that he is missing or dead. All this adds up to a great advantage in a long slogging campaign. But we are asked to envisage, as I have said, a sharp, overwhelming advance; and the very qualities which make the mass of the Soviet army so formidable in a slogging match arise from the primitive nature of the average Russian infantryman, who is a peasant, which is the last thing required in fast-moving warfare.

This means, in effect, that *either* the Soviet army, in attack, may be used as a slow-moving horde, designed to intimidate and then crush the opposition by sheer weight of numbers *or* its armoured spearheads may be used, largely unsupported, for swift-moving enveloping movements: In the first contingency the horde may be cut to pieces by a numerically far inferior mechanized force, coolly handled and fighting with boldness and resolution. In the second contingency the Soviet army loses in the critical phases of the battle its tremendous advantage of sheer size. In both contingencies the actual disparity between the Russians and the forces arrayed against them is seen to be misleading. And it is worth emphasizing in this connection that during the last war the Soviet generals were reluctant to mount an attack until they were assured of a local superiority of six to one.

Even the armoured spearhead, containing the superb élite of the new Soviet army and equipped with tanks as good as any in the world and a great deal better than anything the Western Allies had until almost the end of the war, is not everything it seems. It lacks, notably, adequate communications. It has not begun to catch up on the development of short-wave wireless communications in the field; and this deficiency conditions its whole approach to war. It means that tanks and self-propelled guns are at a distinct disadvantage in a swiftly moving battle. Lack of tank-to-tank wireless means that squadron commanders cannot rapidly adapt their plans to changing situations and tend to fall back on the old cavalry system of follow-my-leader. But tanks have to cover a great deal more ground than cavalry; and the leader may be even less in touch with his superior commander than he is with his individual tank crews.

This problem of communications is proving extremely tiresome for the Soviet High Command. It is not merely a question of providing suitable equipment, although this is difficult in itself, but it is also a question of finding enough men to work and maintain the equipment even when it is available. It is the old story of trying to educate a nation which only thirty years ago was four-fifths peasant, mainly illiterate, and which has had its most enterprising and gifted spirits rigidly suppressed, if not killed off, into being able to fight a modern war with modern and delicate equipment. The men who have in fact been brought on are very good. They fight the tanks, the guns, the tactical aircraft, and the secret weapons. But there are still not enough of them. There are still not enough, for example, to do all this and provide ground and air crews for a really powerful long-distance bombing force. And the gulf between them and the ordinary conscript is still very great. The endurance and frugality of these should be seen as the obverse of their lack of quick intelligence and skill.

All this is not to suggest that the Soviet standing army is anything but a most formidable force. Of course it is formidable. And it is, as I have said, the most powerful asset of the Kremlin. We should need all our might and resolution to match it, and the last thing intended here is to minimize the size of our task. But if we went about it the right way it would be very far from being an impossible task, as many would have us believe it is today. It would not be an impossible task even if the masses behind them and the millions of conscripts who would be called up in time of war could be relied on by Stalin as being heart and soul behind the standing army, which, in fact, they are not.

I have called this chapter "Faster, Faster!" because that describes the tempo of the Soviet Union today. When Stalin decided to launch the Cold War he was opening a war on two fronts, the international front and the home front. He had to force the people of Russia to still greater sacrifices pending the economic collapse of Western Europe, when he would be able to relax. Or, looked at in another way, he was simultaneously pursuing two opposed ends. In obedience to the profound Muscovite tradition he was turning Russia inwards on herself and withdrawing from all contact with the West, while at the same time, in obedience to the newer, Petrine tradition, seeking to impose his will on the West. It was an impossible task. The Soviet Union's self-severance from the rest of the world is in itself something far deeper and more radical than a simple sealing of frontiers. By a surgical operation of extreme elaboration, Stalin is seeking to isolate the consciousness of the Soviet peoples from the living consciousness of humanity as a whole. He has ruthlessly cut through the infinitely complex network of nerves and ligaments and blood vessels which conduct, convey, and apply the common experience and understanding of our civilization. He has cut a whole area from the composite brain of mankind and is trying to turn it into a special Soviet brain. So far so good. Russian rulers have tried to do this before, and they may try again; but what they have never in history attempted to do is to combine this operation with a movement of expansion into that very world which it is so passionately sought to exclude. I myself, as I have already said, do not believe that Stalin, consciously and deliberately, ever intended to thrust deeply into the West. I believe, rather, that the methods he used to achieve what he saw as a simple policy of insulation have, through his violence and stupidity and our own reaction to them, landed him in an intolerable position, which cannot endure for long. Be that as it may, the Cold War for Stalin meant a war on two fronts: a war against his own people and a war against all others. And the prospects of the war against his own people depended on the success of the war against the others.

This, as we have seen, has failed. Instead of a Western Europe in collapse, Stalin is faced with the first stirrings of the mightiest force in the history of the world. And this means that there can be no question at all of any relaxation at home.

During the past three years, the oppressive apparatus of the Kremlin has been employed, above all, against the peasants, who still account for half the total population of the Soviet Union. We have already glanced at the food situation which has made this necessary. Industry, since the revolution, has done relatively well, and the best brains in the Soviet Union have been employed in the service of the industrial revolution, which they have succeeded in turning into a managerial revolution. Agriculture has done less well, and indeed the main effort and the main successes here have been in the development of the so-called industrial crops; cotton above all. But industry cannot continue to do well unless the workers are fed, and the feeding must now be on a better scale than hitherto, because industry has called into being a new type of Russian, doing a new type of work, who can no longer be sustained at his full efficiency by the primitive bread and *kasha* ration on which the Russian peasant or the Russian infantryman can plod his way from the cradle to the grave. The peasants have failed to produce the necessary food; and, because of this, Stalin has been compelled since the beginning of the E.R.P. to launch a new revolution in the countryside, which is no less radical than the collectivization of twenty years ago. It is a revolution designed to bring Soviet agriculture more immediately and completely under central control.

The workers in industry also have to be coerced, but this, up to a point, is a relatively simple matter. It is carried out by the trade unions, so called, which have no similarity at all to the trade unions of the West, but are simply government departments whose task it is to get the most out of the workers for the least reward by making collective agreements over wages, living conditions, and work norms. Factory workers are easy to oversee and to control: the slack, rebellious, or inefficient worker is immediately picked out and jumped on. The agreements made with the trade unions are backed by sanctions, including a form of direction of labour which, although not acknowledged as such, is fairly effective: the man who changes his job forfeits a portion of his social service benefits, including his pension. Lateness and absenteeism are punished by forced labour in its mildest form. The definition of absenteeism is laid down in a decree of the Presidium of the Supreme Soviet of the U.S.S.R. of June 1940: "A Soviet workman is guilty of absenteeism if he loses more than twenty minutes' working time by arriving late, leaving early, or extending his dinner break, or if he commits any of these offences three times in one month or four times in two consecutive months, even if the loss of time in each case is less than twenty minutes." The punishment for this offence may run to "corrective labour without deprivation of freedom" for up to six months. This sentence means that the worker continues at his normal place of employment, but may be ordered to do any work imposed on him and is deprived of up to 25 per cent of his pay. If his offence is repeated, or if he commits more serious offences against industrial discipline, he will be sentenced to one of the heavier categories of forced labour which, according to the Corrective Labour Codex of the R.S.F.S.R., range in severity from corrective labour of a mild kind performed in exile (various categories of exile are laid down) through "corrective labour in a place of detention," including "corrective labour colonies," to "punitive labour colonies"—these last two being the technical term for the labour camps referred to in an earlier chapter. These are the punishments which make it impossible for the Soviet worker, amongst other things, to strike.

The peasants also are subject to this discipline. But, because of the nature of their work in the fields and the impossibility of organizing agricultural production on strictly regimented lines, not all the terror of the M.V.D. can make two blades of grass grow where one grew before. The collectives, with their party administration, were supposed to solve this difficulty, and the "machine tractor stations" were supposed to ensure that the required quantities of grain were delivered to the state. But sooner or later human nature triumphs, and first the collective managers, then the technicians at the machine tractor stations, came to identify themselves with the villagers against the state; while the system of allowing each household an acre and a cow as its own private property, intended originally to keep the peasants in good heart, soon began to threaten the whole fabric of the collective system. Even before the war neglect of work on the collective acres in favour of work on the private plots reached such a pitch that the average peasant was making twice as much from his own small holding as he made from his compulsory work on the collective. During the war the system got completely out of hand, and almost the only food in the towns, apart from a starvation ration, was what the peasants brought in from their private plots and sold on the free market at exorbitant prices. After the war it was found that thousands of collectives all over Russia had been largely broken up by the peasants, with the active connivance of the managers, to increase their own small holdings. And, although the government launched a full-scale campaign to put a stop to these abuses, it found itself powerless to increase the flow of grain into the state granaries. So there followed a series of measures: first the devaluation of the rouble, which was largely aimed at reducing by 90 per cent the hoards of cash accumulated by the peasants; then the agricultural tax, which applied only to earnings from the private holdings, and was, in effect, a punitive tax; then the launching of the great schemes to increase the livestock of the Soviet Union, in size and quantity, a scheme involving the putting down of good arable land to temporary pasture, with the sole purpose of providing more meat and milk for the towns—a scheme bitterly resisted by the Russian peasant, who prefers this year's bread to beef in five years' time; finally the scheme launched by Khruschev in 1950 for the amalgamation of the collectives and for the building of special "agricultural towns." It is this last measure which spells a new revolution, since it means the total breaking down of the old village economy, the end of the private-holding system, and the transformation of the villagers, who have clung so stubbornly to their old customs through all the changes of the last thirty years, into paid employees, or state serfs. They will work in gangs under reliable overseers, and they will live collected together in new settlements, where nobody knows his neighbour, under the direct eye of the party and the police.

The ostensible reason for this revolution is, on the one hand, to turn the smaller collectives into large farms capable of utilizing the most modern farm machinery and, on the other, to move the peasants from their scattered and insanitary villages and house them in brand-new towns with every social and recreational amenity. As far as the smaller collectives are concerned—and many are very small indeed—the machinery argument may seem to have some value; but when we are confronted with the amalgamation of four existing collectives of 7,000 acres each to make one giant farm of 28,000 acres, disposing of only seven combine harvesters and ten tractors (as against 277 draught horses), its real hollowness is clear. As for the enhanced amenities of the agricultural towns, the Russian peasant would rather live in a dugout among his own people and in his own village than be thrown into a regimented barrack life among "foreigners," deprived of the land he has clung to and worked all through the collectivization, no matter how great the amenities.

What this means in practice is a new and deadly phase in the war between the Kremlin and the peasants. The Kremlin is gambling on forcing through this great change, sacrificing some production while it is in progress, for the sake of a greatly increased production in a few years' time, when the resistance to the change is broken and the scheme is under control.

Nobody can tell whether the gamble will succeed. Nobody can tell whether the equally great gamble involved in the great capital development schemes, above all the hydroelectric schemes, will succeed. If they do succeed, then in five to ten years' time the Kremlin will have strengthened and broadened the basis of the Soviet economy sufficiently to solve the question of feeding its vast population once and for all and to divert some of the resources and labour now swallowed up in heavy industry and capital expansion to making consumer goods. But it will be a close-run thing; and if it does not succeed, if the peasants fail to produce more under the new regimentation and the output of undernourished factory workers begins to fall, then the régime will collapse, not as the result of a revolution from below, but as a result of chaos following on a breakdown of the Soviet economy, and the inevitable quarrels in the highest places about what is to be done.

But we need not speculate about the future. What we are concerned with is today. And what I have tried to show is that Stalin has lost the hold he had on the Russian people for a year or so after the war and is in much the same position as he was in 1941, when he feared a war above all things. He has lost his hold because, once more, and largely as a result of his aggressive foreign policy, which has turned half the world against him, he has been forced to drive his all too long-suffering people too far and too hard. And it is a self-accelerating process. Without a great slackening in the international tension he cannot afford to stop. And yet the harder he drives his people the more unreliable will be their mood if it comes to war.

I have dwelt on his problems with the peasants and the workers. These were the problems which also beset him before Hitler's attack—and after. But today he is faced in addition with an entirely new problem: the deterioration of the Communist Party. The Communist Party, as we have seen, was once a devoted band of fanatics, the real vanguard of the proletarian revolution. It grew steadily, in spite of periodic purges, with a developing bias in favour of the growing managerial class. As this development unfolded, again as we have seen, the real power retreated increasingly into the innermost circles of the party, the Central Committee and its standing subcommittees. But the party itself was still devoted to the cause of a Communist Soviet Union until, after the great purge of the middle thirties, which more than decimated its ranks, it largely changed its character: the militant Communists with ideas of their own were removed, as they have since been removed in the Communist Parties of Eastern Europe, and were replaced by timeservers or by young men and women above all interested in serving Stalin as their personal leader. During the war the flower of the younger men (and it was a party predominately young) were killed; but their numbers were more than made up by the simple act of throwing the party open to all gifted and active Soviet patriots who distinguished themselves in any way in the service of the state. Thus, by 1945, the tiny striking force of Leninist fanatics had been entirely transformed into an organized phalanx of the best talent in the Soviet Union, seven million strong, a great proportion of whom paid only lip service to Lenin and to the official ideology. After the war the new party was gently purged and reduced to some six millions, the occupiers of the key positions throughout the land. But still the dilution of ideological consciousness was too great for the party to be effective in its traditional rôle—as the watchdog of the nation's orthodoxy, as the scourge of the apathetic and the disillusioned, and as the inspiration and the discipline of the starry-eyed young. When the time came for the active revival of Leninism it was found that the party could not play its part: it knew all too little of Leninism, and had first to be educated itself before it could begin to educate the people. For year after year since the war the Soviet press has nagged in a steady crescendo at this failure of the party's ideological consciousness. Worse than this, the ever-changing party line, the excesses of the campaign to convince the dull masses that Soviet man was a new sort of man, turning everything he touched into gold, the stupidities of the Kremlin's propagandists and sycophant publicists, the abject contortions of the Soviet intelligentsia in their efforts to follow the changing line, the endless shortages of everything that makes life worth living, the patent lies of the statisticians, the continued severity of police rule—all these have worked together for the disillusionment of the new party. Those who were naturally decent became cynical, profoundly conscious of the gulf between the common people, treated like dirt, and themselves; those who were naturally venal became utterly corrupted. And this alienation between party and government became so great that during the local party congresses of 1949 over half the regional party secretaries were, for one reason or another, deprived of their posts.

Stalin, in transforming the party from a sharp-cutting instrument of like-minded fanatics into a battering ram to carry out his will, had killed the revolutionary spirit. Or, again, in creating his new industrialized state he had created a new and powerful middle class, a strange apparition in Russia. This is an educated body of men and women, whose energies are now divided: the greater part of these energies is now devoted to hanging on to their new privileges at all costs, in constant fear of falling back into the bottomless squalor of the working class from which they have sprung; a lesser part is devoted to making the country work, for sheer pride in seeing it work; while a small but increasing part is developing that critical sense which is the mark of new middle classes everywhere. The Communist Party, except at its highest levels, has become identified with this class. The gulf between the Communist Party of today and its own Central Committee is indicated by the fact that the last party congress, the eighteenth, took place in 1939, twelve years ago, whereas congresses were once held every two or three years. It may scarcely be an exaggeration to say that the gulf between the party and the Kremlin is greater now than the gulf between the party and the people. And it is increasing. For another complaint of the Central Committee, growing in volume and intensity, is that the children are no longer joining the Young Communist League, the Komsomol, in sufficient numbers; and too great a proportion of those who do join regard it only as a kind of social privilege.

For thirty years first Lenin and then Stalin have governed the Soviet Union through the party, backed by all the power of the police. If the party becomes an unreliable instrument, that leaves only the police.

It is hard to tell how much the Russian people can stand without breaking down; certainly they can stand more than the minority nationalities of the Union. These are now troubling the Kremlin so deeply that the radical dilution of these nationalities is being pushed forward at great speed, the natives of the various republics, from Ukraine to Kazakhstan, being moved about and mixed together with the object of destroying each and every focus of national spirit. It is all too easy to think of the Russians in terms of ourselves; and the stories of the refugees from the Soviet Union encourage us in this. It should be clear by now that the Russian unthinkingly accepts deprivations of liberty which we will not accept, and that he can live and flourish in conditions of hardship unthinkable to us. It is also true to say that after so many years of life at its harshest he will accept worse evils than he was ready to accept in 1917. When we are thinking of the appalling conditions of the labour camps, for example, we should remember the appalling conditions of the average Russian village. It is calculated that each village is burned down by fire every five to seven years; and the burning is the spring cleaning. The stench and the dirt and the heat in innumerable Russian homes, hermetically sealed against the killing winter cold, is such that we could not endure it for ten minutes without turning sick. Sometimes, in winter, it becomes too much even for the Russian peasant, who then opens doors and windows and moves into a neighbour's house for two or three days until the frost has killed the vermin. Or, if he can find no one to take him in, he with his wife will simply go out into the forest and stay there for two or three days and nights on end, until the cold has done its sterilizing work. This is the background, either immediate or a generation back, of the Russian prisoners in the labour camps, which kill Poles and Balts and Germans more easily than they kill Russians.

It is also the background to the Kremlin's struggle, which is a genuine struggle, to civilize and discipline the Russian masses. But because of circumstances examined in earlier chapters, and because the speed has been too great, this struggle has defeated its own purpose. It has created a new middle class which will one day supplant the Bolsheviks; but at the same time it has degraded the masses as they were never degraded before. Thus, by a most curious irony, the historical rôle of Lenin and Stalin is turning out to be analogous with the historical rôle of the English capitalists, who produced wealth from degradation and whose successors used that wealth to raise the people out of degradation. In a word, the proletarian revolution in Russia, Lenin's revolution, has had as its one undeniable achievement the creation of a proletariat where none existed before, and the most miserable proletariat in the history of the world.

The degradation is very real, and it is also the Kremlin's most valuable protection. Many times during the war I have seen men and women fall down in the snow, exhausted by starvation, and left lying. They were left lying by people who in their hearts are the kindest people in the world, because nobody had energy to spare to see if they were dead, and because even if they were not dead there was nowhere to take them and no food to give them. That sort of thing is to be expected in times of absolute disaster, disaster on a scale of which we, in England, have had no experience for centuries (for this is what the war meant to Russia). But I also remember—I have the picture, among a dozen others equally catastrophic, clearly before

my eyes—an event which happened two years after the
war, when Russia was recovering. Then, on a main road
quite close to Moscow, an army lorry skidded in the snow.
It ran into a group of women and children and crashed
into a telegraph-pole. The driver was dead in the cab, the
windscreen shattered and splashed with blood; two children lay spread-eagled in the snow, quite dead; an old
woman lay dying by the roadside. The remaining women,
black scarved against the dead-white background, had no
thought for the children; they threw themselves at the
lorry, which was full of army rations, bearing great piles
of food away. They were joined by a mob of women from
neighbouring cottages, who also took no notice of the dead
and dying. Afterwards they would weep; but now they had
food.

Food, of course, is a little easier now; but the corruption
remains. That kind of degradation, and the degradation
of the most generous and spontaneously kindhearted people in the world, is a protection against revolt; but it does
not make good citizens either in peace or in war.

In fact, it is the fear of war, depending upon the ignorance of the Russians, which is Stalin's greatest asset. The
fraudulent peace campaign cuts both ways. It divides the
outside world, as it is designed to do, but equally it
strengthens Stalin's position at home. If he can represent
to millions who know no better that he, backed by the
oppressed and inarticulate millions of the West, can alone
save them from another war, it is very much in his interest
to paint the governments of the West, including Mr.
Attlee's private circus, as hell-bent on war. We have seen
what happened when, in 1947, the Russians were encouraged to think there was an imminent danger of war:
they simply gave up. The new plan is much better, because
the new plan is designed to make the Russian people feel

that, although war is desired by Messrs. Truman, Attlee, and their friends, the masses are powerful enough to prevent it—the oppressed masses of the world, rallying round the Soviet Union, which must be kept together as a bastion of peace by the sacrificial toil of the people of the Soviet Union.

This is one aspect of Stalin's sixth asset, his unscrupulousness.

But the unscrupulous man is never free from the danger of being caught in his own snares. We have seen how this has happened with Stalin in the past, and it will happen again. Unscrupulousness is not, in any case, a quality for envy.

It may seem to some that I have exaggerated the case against the Soviet régime. I do not think I have: there was a period, after the war, when, by setting a new course, Stalin, despite his dreadful past, might have saved the spirit of his people. I myself believed there was a very good chance of his doing so; and I hoped that he would do so, because the Russians had suffered too much, and it was a terrible thought that it might have been in vain. He has not done so; and perhaps, indeed, he had no choice, being sunk too deep in tyranny to draw back, even in his own personal interest.

Others will indignantly deny the truth of this picture (it is only a part of the picture; but they will deny that it is even that). The Soviet Union, they will say, is strong and prospering and fearless. I don't know why people who have been to Russia, or even read about it, say these things —unless they are deliberately lying for purposes of their own or for the purposes of Stalin. Do they never ask themselves how, if the Soviet régime is as secure and prosperous as they make out, the Kremlin can have a vestige of excuse for its behaviour outside Russia?

Others still ask why, if things are as bad as I have said, there are not more refugees, more desertions from the Soviet army and missions serving abroad. I have tried to show that hatred of the régime is not a new thing to the Russians, and does not lead to immediate, reasoned action. Love of country, too, runs very deep, and this we should understand. I once asked a Russian woman who had known of the West at least by hearsay, who came of a military family respected under the tsars, who regarded the régime with a sombre, hard, and unforgiving hatred, who had nothing visible to live for—I once asked this woman of thirty-five, who had learned to speak Petrograd French from a palace governess and whose life had been one long disaster, whether, if she could, she would leave Russia never to return. With only the slightest hesitation she said, decisively, that she would not—in spite of everything. And when I asked why not she looked away to the forest and said, "But how could I leave the birch trees? . . ."

Many, of course, in the days of the tsars, did leave the birch trees—and the steppe. Many more would leave today. But those who try to cross the frontier are shot, and those soldiers who are tempted to desert while serving in Germany and Austria have perpetually before their eyes the decree of the Supreme Soviet, which tells them in the simplest language that the whole family of any soldier who deserts while serving abroad will be sentenced to five years' corrective labour "in the remote regions of Siberia."

5. *Final Reflections*

Final Reflections

We HAVE GOT SO FAR in this book without asking the question: will there be war? This must be a record. My own deep conviction that there will not be a major war with Russia, at least in this generation, is based on the conclusions reached at one time and another in the preceding chapters. That is to say, I do not believe that Stalin will start a war of conquest. The dangers that we may stumble into war as a result of diplomatic ineptitude and ill-will and panic are, of course, obvious. But I hope I have said enough to show that there is no analogy at all between Stalin and Russia, on the one hand, and Hitler and Germany, on the other. Stalin, as we have seen, has no moral objection to war, and the course he is engaged in now is as evil as any war of conquest. But it is not a war of conquest. Stalin has none of Hitler's compulsion to go to war; indeed, the compulsion is all the other way, taking into consideration his own nature, the categories of Marxist thinking, Soviet geography and resources, the nature of the Russian people, and the miserable and unreliable state of the Soviet Union today. There seems to me only one possible reason for Stalin to go to war, and that is to achieve by force of arms the destruction of the European economy which he has so far failed to achieve by

273

other methods. If he could do this without suffering fearful retribution he might conceivably do so; but nobody who saw Moscow in the autumn of 1941 could believe for one moment that the Soviet Union could hold together under American bombing. This is the argument of those who say that possession of the atom bomb is the sole deterrent to Soviet attack. I myself do not believe this. For reasons already suggested, I think that, in the first place, Stalin does not desire a war of conquest and that even if he wished to launch a preventive war the Soviet economy, for some years to come, would be unable to stand the strain of total mobilization.

This does not mean that we should not be prepared for attack. Opinions are opinions, and I have tried to indicate the basis of mine. But the Cold War and Stalin's lack of inhibitions about aggressive war in principle are facts; and we have to take notice of them. In the long run it may be only our power to resist which will keep the Soviet Union within bounds until such time as, by whatever means, her new middle class reaches maturity and either seizes control of the government in catastrophe and reverses its whole policy or else gradually, and with the passage of time, by increasing influence and pressure, itself becomes the government. But we cannot wait on this, which means that, whether we like it or not, we have to waste money on armaments which we could spend more happily on other things.

But is "waste" really the word? Soviet Russia is a fact of life, like any other—like, for example, the weather. We do not spend our time and energy shaking our fists at the clouds: we buy an umbrella, and we do not regard the money spent as waste. One of the tragedies of our time is that we seem unable to accept the cost of arming until we have lashed ourselves into a hysteria of fear and hatred.

It is only because of this that the saying about armaments leading inevitably to war is likely to be true; it is not the arms that lead to war, but the feeling behind them. And the feeling behind them, the hatred and the fear, is not, when one comes to look at it, hatred and fear of the enemy; it is hatred of life itself, which demands these sacrifices. I do not hate the badger that lives in the wood at the bottom of my garden and suddenly, reprehensibly, develops a taste for my chickens. He costs me time and money which could be better spent (on what?); but, when he is safely wired out, I continue to admire him as a handsome and amiable beast whose interests regrettably come into conflict with mine. If he breaks through the wire or burrows under it, so that I cannot keep him out, well, he will have to be killed. He can be killed, because I am the stronger. But there will be no hatred, only regret, in my heart. And with luck the wire will keep him out, so that he will not have to be killed—wire bought, without rancour, with nothing but a sad recognition of the hard facts of life, with money which was to have bought—well, anything but wire for keeping badgers out of chicken runs. It seems to me that a little of this spirit in our attitude to some of the larger facts of life would do us all no harm.

These are trite reflections; but they are the natural response to an essentially trite situation which we have succeeded in dramatizing beyond its deserts. It is a situation which has repeated itself without a pause since the beginning of the world. And I would ask my American friends, who think that we in this island are taking it too lightly, to reflect that we have had to live with the idea of invasion, and sometimes the fact, for the last two thousand years.

Then there are those who think that communism is preferable to war. In the history of the world there have been many revolutions and we ourselves are a product of them all. Yet today we find ourselves in the frame of mind in which we are able to contemplate the total destruction of the civilized world, including our own country, rather than permit the fulfilment of the Communist revolution. We, as the products of history, may fairly say that the defeat of no past revolution was worth this sacrifice. What is it about the advance of what we call communism which puts it into a different category from all the revolutionary movements of the past? I hope this book will have provided the answer to that question: it is not communism as an internal revolutionary movement that we are preparing to resist with all the hideous paraphernalia of modern warfare; it is the government of a foreign power bent on undermining our own society and, if it comes to war, on replacing it with its own system, which we find an evil system. The only sort of people who may decently refuse to resist such an onslaught are those who believe that all resistance to force is evil, presumably basing their attitude on the belief that force, having nothing to feed on, will wither away—or, in concrete terms, that by total surrender, even to our physical destruction, we shall become the agents of Stalin's purification. I do not believe this; and I feel certain that the vast majority of those who advocate today a policy of neutrality do not believe it either. They advocate neutrality not because they think it wicked to resist evil by force, but because they feel that evil will win. That is a point of view; but it is not our problem. It is a problem for God, if he exists; and if he does not, then it does not arise.

"Les imbéciles ont toujours raison." That was Clemenceau's phrase, and there is a good deal in it. We notice it in the bewilderment shown by millions of ordinary men and women all over Europe which is so easily exploited

by the Politburo in their own interests, above all in the notorious perversion of the universal desire for peace. A great many people found themselves incapable of with-holding their signatures from a simple and apparently in-nocuous document demanding the outlawing of atomic warfare. The people, the imbeciles, as Clemenceau called them, are perfectly right to be bewildered, if only because so much that is talked about Russia by responsible leaders, noted for their intelligence, is obviously wrong— obviously wrong even to those who have no direct knowledge of the truth. And in addition there are the counterpressures set up by our intellectual leaders.

We live, says Mr. Burnham, in a catastrophic age. "The totalitarian political movements of our century, particu-larly the Communist, have accepted a catastrophic point of view." He then proceeds to tell us that if we do not also accept the catastrophic point of view, fight the Com-munists with their own weapons, and regard the sort of experience we have undergone during the last forty years as normal rather than exceptional, we are lost. But the whole deep error of Mr. Burnham lies in that single, harm-less-looking sentence. The totalitarians have not *accepted* the catastrophic point of view; they have *created* it, and, through eager disciples like Mr. Burnham, they are trying to impose it on us. Mr. Burnham was born with it, and so was Mr. Koestler. Both now try to whip us up into an active crusade against communism, using communism's weapons. Both are ex-Communists, who revolted against Stalin. Both, that is to say (and how many more besides), sought short cuts to impossible ends, to a world different, and also, they believed, much better, than the world we live in. Both were frustrated. Both are still seeking short cuts through violence and trying to drag us with them. And it never occurs to either of them, or to the thousands who think like them, that what they are really denouncing is not communism or fascism, or this or that manifestation of humanity, but life itself—life which will not do what it is told. The Koestlers and the Burnhams, the frustrated totalitarians, are not anti-Communist; fundamentally, they are antihumanity. But, not content, like Madame du Deffand, to leave it at that, or unable to realize the truth of their condition, they seek to plunge the world into a militant crusade, for one reason alone: to recover their own lost faith.

At the other extreme, though on a less spectacular level, are those Left-wing Socialists, and others, who try to pretend that the Soviet system would be, for us, no worse than the American system. My own reasons for believing that the Soviet system is not only worse than the American system but also positively evil, whereas the American system is at least potentially good, have been given in this book; and I shall not labour the comparison. Few people, I suppose, have a greater admiration and affection for the Russian people than I have; and if I have treated them roughly in these pages (which offer only one small aspect of the truth) I have shown elsewhere not only admiration and affection but also the conviction that one day, sooner or later, the world will be grateful to them for keeping intact certain values which we have lost. Few people, I suppose, opposed to the Soviet system have tried harder than I have to show the accidental quality of its worst excesses, including even, I believe, the Cold War—accidental, that is to say, as opposed to calculated and deliberate, though arising inevitably from the rejection of certain values which cannot, I believe, be rejected with impunity. Few people, I suppose, are more sharply critical than I am of certain aspects of the American way of life, of the way in which Americans seem incapable of realizing their own strength, and of the extent to which they are unconsciously imposing their way of life on the nations of Western Europe, or of the way in which, for example, American fiscal and tariff policy has contributed to the breakdown of the West. But if it comes to the choice between America and Russia there simply is no choice. For better or for worse the "we" defined in the first chapter of this book includes the vast majority of Englishmen and Western Europeans and Americans. We believe, fundamentally, in the same values, though, heaven knows, those values are often distorted and almost lost; and they are the values which Stalin is out to kill. It is as simple as that. We do not have to admire each individual characteristic of our friends, nor they of us. But we know who are our friends.

I can think of only one way in which the Kremlin may still conquer us, and that without war. It is by so frightening us (but it is we who allow ourselves to be frightened) that for fear of the enemy within we transform our own society imperceptibly into an apparatus of totalitarianism indistinguishable in essence from the society of Soviet Russia—a system which may not be criticized, whether the British parliamentary system or the American way of life, for fear of damaging national unity, the unity of the grave; a system in which the bully and the corrupt may not be denounced or the underdog uplifted because nobody will dare risk being called a Red. This, it seems to me, is a very real danger. Already in Western Europe and America, but above all in America, the Communists have been allowed to monopolize the advocacy of a fair number of desirable reforms. Should the day come when we are afraid to pursue each and every enlightened course of action because the Communists, for their own deplorable reasons, are associated with them too, then Stalin will have won.

Acknowledgments

Some of the material in this book has been the subject of articles in *The National and New English Review, The New Statesman and Nation, The Listener, The Observer,* and *International Affairs,* the quarterly journal of the Council of the Royal Institute of International Affairs, to the editors of which I owe thanks. I am indebted, too, to Mr. Isaac Deutscher for kindly allowing me to quote from his book *Stalin: A Political Biography,* published by the Oxford University Press. My general obligation to historians and scholars who have specialized in Russian and Soviet studies is unbounded.

E. C.